Lois Hole's
Vegetable Favorites

To My Mother,
Elsa Veregin
who instilled in me a love of gardening.

The Publisher: Lone Pine Publishing

206, 10426 – 81 Ave.	202A, 1110 Seymour St.	1901 Raymond Ave. SW, Suite C
Edmonton, AB	Vancouver, BC	Renton, WA
T6E 1X5 Canada	V6B 3N3 Canada	98055 USA

Canadian Cataloguing in Publication Data
Hole, Lois, 1933–
    Lois Hole's vegetable favorites

(Lois Hole's gardening guides)
Includes index.
Previous ed. has title: Lois Hole's northern vegetable gardening.
ISBN 1-55105-072-2

1. Vegetable gardening—Canada. I. Title. II. Title: Vegetable favorites.
III. Title: Lois Hole's northern vegetable gardening. IV. Series: Hole, Lois,
1933– Lois Hole's gardening guides.
SB321.H64 1996   635'.0971   C96-910058-2

Design and Layout: Bruce Timothy Keith
Cover Design: Carol S. Dragich
Editorial: Debby Shoctor
Illustrations: Horst H. Krause
  Printing: Select Colour Press, Edmonton, Alberta, Canada
Photo Credits: Akemi Matsubuchi cover, 22, 23, 24, 54, 78, 81, 85, 120, 129, 135;
  Jill Fallis 112, 135; B. Miokovic / The Mach 2 Stock Exchange Ltd. 91;
  Wayne Shiels / Photo Search Ltd. 106; All-America Selections 116.
  Thank you to Alberta Agriculture, Ball Seed Co., and Stokes Seeds Ltd.
  for their assistance in providing photographs.

The publisher gratefully acknowledges the assistance of the Federal Department
of Communications, Alberta Community Development, the Canada Council,
and the financial support provided by the Alberta Foundation for the Arts, in the
production of this book.

CONTENTS

꧁ ☙ ❧ ꧂

ACKNOWLEDGEMENTS

My sincere thanks to Jill Fallis for her invaluable contribution to me in the research and writing of this book; to my family, Ted, Bill, Jim and Valerie Hole, for helping me out in innumerable ways; and to the editorial and design staff of Lone Pine Publishing for all their hard work.

A special thanks to those who toiled with us in the garden over the years, and in particular to the late Mrs. Virginia Durocher. Thanks also to Lloyd Hauser and Paul Ragan of the Brooks Research Centre, and to the staff of the Alberta Tree Nursery & Horticultural Centre, for the indispensable information made available through their vegetable trials.

FOREWORD

Ever since I was a little girl, I have loved gardening. My mother grew the largest garden in our small Saskatchewan town, and she allowed me to help, pulling weeds, picking and shelling peas. It was never something that I was made to do, but rather a pleasure in which I was pemitted to share.

In the years since, I have had many wonderful experiences in gardening, particularily in the business of growing vegetables. Over the past 20 years, I have attempted to share some of my knowledge, experience and love of growing, by giving talks on gardening to various audiences, such as school children, farm women, church groups, senior's clubs, both men's and women's organizations, the Devonian Botanic Garden and the John Jantzen Nature Centre. The common thread in this diverse collection of people is their interest in gardening.

This book has been written for all those who share the love of gardening.

PREFACE

IN THE BEGINNING

Vegetable gardening is much more than the enjoyment of eating freshly-picked peas, or tomatoes right off the vine. I get immense satisfaction from setting seeds in the bare earth, seeing the green shoots emerge, and tending young plants through to glorious maturity.

My husband Ted and I.

Ted and I got our start in vegetable farming in the early 1950s, when we bought 200 acres of fertile land just a few miles from the village of St. Albert, Alberta and set out to grow grain and raise cattle, pigs, chickens and turkeys. Ted had a university degree in agriculture, but neither of us had a farming background, nor had we ever lived on a farm. We soon discovered that one of the best ways to learn is from the experience of others, and that belief holds true to this day. People who have shared information with us on everything from labour-saving devices to new plant varieties have contributed immensely to our knowledge and success. The joy of discovery is what keeps the adventure in gardening and fuels the love of growing.

We started our first vegetable garden next to the house, largely out of necessity rather than for pleasure. The garden was only about 30 yards (27m) from the road that ran next to our house, and people out for leisurely drives through the country began to stop and ask if they could buy our vegetables. I always grew more than I needed — a common folly of the farm wife — and was happy to sell the extra vegetables from our back door. The interest of those first customers sparked our enthusiasm for vegetable growing, and Ted and I decided that this was something that could really work. More space and time was dedicated to raising vegetables, until that became our primary focus.

DOOR-TO-DOOR VEGETABLE SALES

One summer I came up with the idea of selling the extra vegetables at an apartment block in the city. I filled the back of our old pick-up truck with fresh produce, strapped in our sons Bill and Jim, then about four and three years old, and headed off. On the first trip, I knocked on apartment doors, and soon sold all that I had. From that day forward, there was such a demand for vegetables that people would watch for the truck to arrive, and I never had enough to match the demand.

We also sold fresh vegetables to many of the big hotels in the city during those early years. First thing in the morning, we would head out to pick potatoes, head lettuce, cabbage, slicing cucumbers and garden peas, and load our harvest into the truck for delivery by noon. Sometimes our neighbour Mary Sernowski would come along to watch the boys while I delivered the vegetables to the kitchens of Edmonton's grand Hotel MacDonald, among other places.

One year we placed a small classified advertisement in the city newspaper, just two lines: *Vegetables for sale, Hole's. Telephone 599-8579.* The phone rang off the hook. We were amazed at the number of people who arrived at our farm on weekends, in search of huge amounts of fresh vegetables. Large Italian families would disappear into the fields and emerge an hour later with hundreds of pounds of peas, green beans and broad beans. We sold potatoes in 100-pound sacks, and people with large families would buy as many as 20 sacks at one time to last through the winter.

THE INTERNATIONAL INFLUENCE

In those days the average Canadian family ate only the traditional vegetables: peas, corn and potatoes. The biggest demand came from the ethnic communities: Italians, Pakistanis, Lebanese, East Indians and many others who also introduced us to many international culinary delights. Until their arrival, we had never heard of eggplant or patty pan squash, or tasted a meal flavoured with chili peppers and garlic.

My son Bill next to the bean harvester. Handpicking still resulted in the best-quality crop.

Italians introduced us to zucchini, broccoli and paste tomatoes; the Lebanese told us about *cousa*, a young vegetable marrow squash. We learned about marvellous types of peppers and all kinds of squashes, and the world of flavours provided by fresh herbs.

People brought us recipes — all sorts of wonderful recipes. We sold tomatoes green in the years that the weather did not promote ripening, and I discovered how to make use of the unripened fruit.

Things did not always go smoothly. One summer I was in the hospital having a baby, Ted was trying to run the farm on his own and the weeds in the summer fallow grew so high they had to be mowed down and plowed under. Another year, our hired man accidentally started the straw roof of our root cellar on fire. We were very fortunate when times were tough, to have selfless neighbours, the Bococks and Rosses, to help us rebuild and get back on our feet.

Overall we were extremely fortunate. The weather was good and we had a beautiful growing area beside the house which gave us lovely crops. One summer, a young girl about 13 years old came out to ask if she could work in the fields picking vegetables. We hired her and drove her up to the far fields, telling her someone would be back in a couple of hours to get her. That afternoon while Ted was fixing the tractor, the jack broke and the tractor fell on him, breaking his leg quite badly. The whole family rushed him to the hospital, and hours later Valerie walked down from the fields to find the farm deserted. She walked two miles (3 km) back to town, and swore that she would never go back. But her mother told her to never quit a job on the first day. Valerie found out the next day what had happened, and she has not only worked for us ever since, she is now Bill's wife and manages the greenhouses.

My favourite job in the greenhouses is watering the growing plants.

Greenhouses were a natural extension — in the relatively short growing season of northern areas, it makes sense to give some plants a head start. We built a plastic-covered greenhouse to house some of the vegetables, and when customers began to ask if they could buy plants from our greenhouses, we knew that home gardeners shared our desire to extend the growing season and reap an earlier harvest.

Anyone who has grown a vegetable garden knows that it can be an immensely enjoyable experience, yet equally frustrating at times. It's the frustrating part of vegetable growing that has inspired me to write this book. Often the disappointment that we all experience at one time or another in the garden can largely be avoided by simply understanding the basic requirements of each crop. I've written this book with a strong emphasis on the basics of vegetable gardening and I've also included lots of tips and illustrations to make growing simple. It is my hope that this book will provide the information you need to produce the tastiest, highest-yielding vegetables possible with a minimal amount of effort.

Third-generation gardeners Michael and Kathryn Hole.

THE VEGETABLE GARDEN

Vegetables can be grown in a traditional garden plot, in large patio containers, or intermingled in a flower bed. Even a small garden can produce a large amount of vegetables, if you choose the right crops and gardening methods.

LOCATION

There are three basic requirements for a vegetable garden:

A field of potatoes in a river valley (early to mid-June).

A sunny location. Vegetables need at least six hours of direct sunlight each day; the more sun they receive, the greater the harvest and the better their taste. Only small vegetables such as radishes or leaf lettuce will do reasonably well in areas that are somewhat shady.

A rich, well-drained soil. Vegetables that are grown in rich soil will be large and tasty, while those grown in poor soil will be weak and more prone to disease and insect attacks.

Space. The amount of space needed to grow vegetables varies from crop to crop. For example, corn needs a lot of space, and can overshadow shorter crops. You can either choose to omit this vegetable in a small garden, or to grow it alongside crops tolerant of light shade.

If you have only a limited area available for a vegetable garden, then be creative. Try mixing flowers and vegetables in the garden. Plant tomatoes and asparagus in the flower bed; use carrots for a leafy border. Many vegetables will flourish in containers. See *Specialty Vegetable Gardens* for ideas and details.

WHAT TO GROW

What to grow depends mainly on why you are growing it. Do you want a ready supply of your favourite vegetable — rosy, vine-ripened tomatoes; tender, fresh peas-in-the-pod; juicy, sweet corn-on-the-cob? I like peas, so they always get a large area in my garden. If you love salads, then grow lots of lettuce, but be innovative in your methods. Experiment with a French method of salad gardening (see page 30) for a *salade de mesclun*, or mix different varieties of leaf lettuce for a colourful display in the garden and a beautiful salad on the table.

If you are growing vegetables to have a continuous supply on hand for long-term use, plant those that store well. A crop such as asparagus, which must be used as soon as it matures and which requires a fair amount of garden space, may not be for you. If you live in an area with a short growing season, choose early-maturing varieties of vegetables, or reduce the time to maturity by starting transplants indoors.

TRYING NEW VARIETIES

Every year seed companies come out with new vegetable varieties. Be willing to experiment. The new varieties often have a greater resistance to pests and produce better quality fruit. Each year we test several new varieties of vegetables in our garden. These *trial* plants are graded on their performance under various weather conditions — heavy rain, or hot, dry periods — and on how early they reach maturity. If the new vegetables perform exceptionally well in the field tests, and pass the taste test at the dinner table, they are placed on our recommended list.

Trying new things — whether it's testing new varieties, different methods of growing, or simply trying a new vegetable — adds to the fun of gardening.

The Best Vegetables for Storing

These vegetables will keep for the longest time, under ideal conditions:
Beets, Carrots, Potatoes, Pumpkins, Rutabaga, Squash (winter types).
Refer to sections on the individual vegetables for the
best methods of storage.

HOW MUCH TO PLANT

Plant only as much as can be consumed while the crop is at its peak. The purpose of growing your own vegetables is to enjoy them at their freshest, with that *just-picked* flavour.

During the enthusiasm of spring planting, it is sometimes hard to refrain from simply running down the row until the seed packet is empty, but try to imagine this: one packet of lettuce can contain hundreds of seeds! It is far better to sow a lesser amount every few weeks for a continuous supply of fresh, tender leaves through the summer, than to have a large supply of lettuce ready all at once.

I always sow seed more thickly than many experts recommend, to ensure a good stand even if some plants are lost to frost or pests. Few gardeners have the expertise, time and luck needed to produce a perfect stand of vegetables. Always assume that some seeds are not going to survive to maturity, and plant accordingly.

The Easiest Vegetables to Grow

These vegetables can be grown from seed, are easy to sow, mature
quickly, require no staking or pruning, are most resistant to
pests and frost, and are easy to harvest:
Beans, Beets, Lettuce (leaf), Peas, Potatoes, Radishes, Spinach.

How much time do you have for the garden? Gardening should be a joy, not a chore. Determine how much time you want to devote to your garden, and plant within those limits. Anything grown from seed will require daily watering at the seedling stage; certain varieties of tomatoes will need staking and pruning; and peas and beans will need to be picked almost daily to prevent them from becoming tough and seedy. If you are away often, or have little time to spend in your garden, it may be wise to avoid a crop such as celery, which requires extra effort.

WHEN TO PLANT

The standard advice to gardeners is to plant once danger of frost is passed. Check with your local weather office for the average *frost-free* growing period for your area. In general, once the leaves are out on native trees, it means that the area is safe from hard frosts until fall.

Determine when it is generally *safe* to plant in your area, but do not succumb to the idea of a *magical* safe-planting date. Many people wait until Victoria Day, for example, to plant the garden. In some years, however, the weather allows planting earlier; in other years, you may have to wait until early June to set out tender crops. Learn which types of vegetables can withstand light frosts, and take a chance on an earlier harvest by planting early in the spring.

Vegetables that are started from seed can generally be planted earlier than seedlings transplanted into the gardens. Some crops can also be sown in the fall.

Many vegetables can be sown several times in a growing season. Multiple seedings ensure that at least one seeding produces a crop if the growing conditions are poor, or provide a continuous crop of nice-sized vegetables when the growing conditions are good. Radishes and lettuce are good examples of vegetables that are suited to multiple seedings. In the spring, they can be sown as soon as the soil is workable, and again every week thereafter until early July.

MICROCLIMATES

Microclimates are distinct areas within a climatic zone that exhibit significant variations with respect to the surrounding areas. Microclimates vary from garden to garden. For example, frost comes earlier to valleys because cold air pools at the bottom of hills. If you live at the top of a hill and have a sheltered garden, you will probably have more success with early plantings than your neighbour who lives down the hill near the river.

Between the rows of trees and two corn patches, a miniature microclimate has been created. The garden patch in the middle is perfect for heat-loving crops.

Some vegetables, such as lettuce, spinach and cauliflower prefer cool weather, while others such as tomatoes, peppers and melons, love heat. By adapting your gardening practices to your particular garden, you will increase your chances of success. The glory of the harvest is, after all, what vegetable gardening is all about.

Vegetables Most Tolerant of Frost

Some vegetables can withstand several degrees of frost without damage. Among these are cabbage, cauliflower, celery, onions, peas, potatoes, spinach, and Swiss chard. The flavour of vegetables like Brussels sprouts, carrots, parsnips, rutabaga and turnips actually improves after a light fall frost!

Potato foliage is sensitive to frost; however, new leaves rapidly grow to replace those that are damaged. Tubers are unaffected by frost if they are thoroughly covered in soil.

Spring Schedule of Earliest Outdoor Planting

In general, vegetables can be categorized as hardy, tender, or heat-loving. This chart provides an overall guide to spring-planting dates for vegetables, but refer to the individual sections for more specific information on each vegetable.

Approximate date of last spring frost in your area: _____.

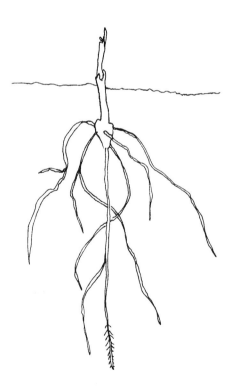

Hardy Vegetables

Plant up to 5 weeks before last frost:
Asparagus, Beets, Broccoli, Brussels sprouts, Cabbage, Carrots, Cauliflower, Celeriac, Celery, Garlic, Kale, Kohlrabi, Leeks, Lettuce, Onions, Parsnips, Peas, Potatoes, Radishes, Rutabaga, Spinach, Swiss chard, Turnips.

Tender Vegetables

Plant on or just prior to last frost:
Beans, Corn, Zucchini.
Small corn plants can survive a frost because the growing point is below the soil surface.

Heat-loving Vegetables

Plant 1 to 2 weeks after last frost:
Cucumbers, Eggplant, Melons, Peppers, Pumpkins, Squash, Tomatoes.
Except for cucumbers and squash, these should be transplanted rather than seeded into the garden.

Growing point of corn.

FROST

It is not uncommon to suffer an unseasonable frost in northern areas — even in mid-August. Cover anything susceptible to frost damage if you are not prepared to take a chance. Use old sheets, blankets, towels, burlap or even a cardboard box. Never cover with plastic; it has virtually no insulation value.

Snow in the spring or fall usually does not harm plants, but instead acts as an insulator, like a blanket. Only be concerned about snow if it is very heavy and wet; its weight can cause some plants to break.

Kale is one of the most frost-tolerant vegetables.

Beating the Frost

One season when our corn plants were about 2 inches (5 cm) high and the cucumbers were really growing well, we had a horrendous frost in early June. The corn died down to ground level but quickly began to regrow, because the growing point of corn plants remains protected below the soil surface for several weeks after the plants emerge. The frost did kill the cucumbers, but we replanted and ended up with a particularly good crop. Frost-damaged vegetables are not fit for eating. Vegetables such as beans, corn, cucumbers, pumpkins, squash, tomatoes and zucchini are most susceptible to damage by even a light frost. Soft-shelled, young squashes and pumpkins may be damaged; hard shells will protect the fruit.

GARDEN LAYOUT

When planning the garden, consider the space requirements of different vegetables at various stages of growth. Corn, for example, will overshadow shorter crops, so those vegetables that tolerate lightly shaded areas are good choices for the neighbouring rows. Other crops require a great deal of growing room; if your garden space is limited, you might choose to omit these vegetables, or to grow them vertically (see *Gardening in Small Spaces*).

Vegetables that are Tolerant of Light Shade

Areas that are partially shaded will support these crops; production will be less prolific than in a sunnier area, but the plants are less likely to *bolt* to seed in the heat of the summer:
Leaf Lettuce, Spinach, Swiss chard.

Vegetables that Require a Lot of Space

These vegetables can take up a lot of room in the garden. Most have spreading vines. Allow them generous amounts of room, or, if possible, choose *bush* varieties, which have a more compact habit of growth:
Corn, Cucumbers, Melons, Pumpkins, Squash.

CROP ROTATION

Crop rotation is the practice of changing the location of vegetables in the garden from year to year. For example, peas might be planted in the northeast corner of the garden one year, and then planted in the southeast corner the next . The purpose of crop rotation is to reduce the incidence of soil-inhabiting pests by removing their preferred food source. It is important to rotate not only an individual crop but also any other vegetables in the same botanical family. Rotation works best if the crops that are particularly prone to pest problems are moved as far away as possible from their location the previous season. It is best to wait at least three years before replanting in the original area.

Crop rotation is also practised to make the best use of the soil. Corn and celery, for example, are *heavy feeders:* they require a lot of nutrients, and grow extremely well in a rotation with peas or beans. Peas and beans are *legumes* which collect nitrogen on their roots and release it to the soil. Since heavy feeders like corn and celery need a lot of nitrogen, this rotation is ideal.

In a very small garden, crop rotation is practical only if you have experienced a severe problem with a certain pest in one or more growing seasons.

SUCCESSION CROPPING

Succession cropping is another method of gardening which works well in a limited space. This is the practice of planting more than one crop in the same garden space or row, with the second crop planted after the first has been harvested: for example, early leaf lettuce can be followed by bush beans.

As with intercropping, you must consider the time to maturity. In general, quick-growing crops are followed by later-maturing crops.

INTERCROPPING

In a small garden, intercropping can result in greater yields. Intercropping means planting two or more crops at the same time in the same patch of ground or in the same row. For example, radish seed can be mixed with that of slower-growing vegetables like carrots or parsnips, and crops of cabbage or cauliflower can be planted between rows of earlier-maturing vegetables such as Swiss chard or spinach. As you harvest the first crop, room is left for the later crops to mature.

With intercropping, you must consider the time to maturity and space requirements of the vegetables at various stages of growth. In general, small, quick-growing crops can be planted with larger, slower-maturing ones, or next to vining or spreading vegetables.

Nutrient Requirements of Vegetables

Vegetables vary in the amounts of nutrients they require. The following chart lists vegetables by their relative consumption of the major nutrients: nitrogen, phosphorous and potassium.

- *Light feeders* require less nutrients;
- *Medium feeders* require more nutrients;
- *Heavy feeders* require the most nutrients.

SOIL

Composition

The best vegetables are grown in a soft, rich, well-drained soil. In a loam soil (the ideal garden soil), air and roots can easily penetrate and nutrients are readily available.

Adding lots of humus (decomposed organic matter) each year ensures the soil remains loose and allows roots to grow properly. It will also minimize problems with *crusting*, a condition that makes it difficult if not impossible for the sprouts of small-seeded vegetables such as carrots, onions and lettuce to push through the hard surface.

Few gardens contain soil that is *perfect* for vegetable production. In other areas of your garden, you may be able to get away without amending the soil by choosing trees, shrubs and flowers that thrive in less than ideal conditions, but you cannot get away with it in a vegetable garden. Continually *building* the soil will ensure lush, healthy crops which have a greater resistance to insects and disease.

The first step is determining what type of soil you have. Here is an easy way to do this: scoop up moist soil in your hand, squeeze your hand into a fist, then open your hand to examine the soil. If you can see the imprint of your fingers and the soil stays in a ball, even when poked, then you have clay soil. If it falls away as you open your hand, it is a sandy soil. If it stays compact but falls easily apart into small clumps when poked, then you are fortunate. This is likely a loam soil that has the ideal balance of sand, silt, clay and humus.

Well-drained soil is neither too dry nor too wet, but instead maintains the optimum balance between air and water. Soils that have poor drainage become soggy and bog-like, resulting in poor root growth and smaller yields. Soils that drain too easily become dry very quickly and are usually lower in nutrients.

Soil pH

The ability of plants to absorb nutrients depends, to a large extent, on the soil pH. This is a scale from 1 to 14 which measures acidity (low pH) and alkalinity (high pH). Vegetables grow best in slightly acidic soil, at a pH of about 6.5.

If the pH of the soil is too high or too low, nutrient absorption is adversely affected, and yields will be lower. Generally, most soils have a pH in the correct range and testing is only necessary if plants exhibit poor growth.

If you suspect a pH problem, take a soil sample in to your local garden centre, or check the yellow pages of your telephone directory for companies that provide soil-testing services. Follow their recommendations for amendments.

How to Improve Soil

All soils benefit from the regular addition of organic matter. Organic matter opens clay soil, making it easier for air and roots to penetrate, and binds sandy soil so it dries out slower. Organic matter also nourishes the beneficial microorganisms that live in soil, and improves its capacity to store nutrients.

Good garden soil is a balance of sand, silt, clay and organic matter. It is light, allows air and water to penetrate, and roots to easily grow and obtain adequate nourishment and moisture. An application of organic matter is important to ensure soil productivity. Well-rotted manure, compost and peat moss are good examples of quality organic matter.

Peat Moss is generally extracted from bogs, and sold in compressed bales. Peat moss is an excellent material to loosen the soil and hold water; however, it is quite acidic. If you add a large quantity of peat moss to a pH-balanced soil, be sure to neutralize the acidity with garden limestone.

Composted Manure is also called well-rotted manure; it is dry, crumbly and virtually odourless. Cows and sheep are the most common sources; sheep manure is often more expensive because it is richer in plant nutrients. Never apply fresh manure to the garden; it can burn plants and will encourage root crops such as carrots to become hairy and bitter.

After several years of gardening, you should have a large supply of organic matter in the compost bin. Composting is an excellent way to recycle nutrient-rich organic matter. It also reduces the amount of material sent to the landfill, and is generally very inexpensive to maintain.

Composting

Composting is simply a method of accelerating the natural decomposition of a wide range of organic materials, to produce **humus** (decomposed organic matter). Compost is wonderful for the home gardener because it enhances the texture of the soil, and adds beneficial microorganisms and nutrients, as well as improving drainage.

The correct balance of organic matter, air and water is needed to make compost. Choose a composter that is large enough for your needs and that retains sufficient moisture, while allowing good air movement throughout.

The compost material should be about as wet as a damp sponge, on average, and the pile should be turned over once in a while. Turning the pile allows air to penetrate, providing oxygen for the microorganisms which do the work of decomposition, and prevents the pile from smelling.

The easiest way to get started is to buy a ready-made compost bin; however, you may choose to construct your own. Some people simply compost in a pile rather than a bin; however, bins are neater and encourage more rapid decomposition than piles. Lids keep out animals and rain; too much rain inhibits proper decomposition and results in a waterlogged, soggy mess.

Things That Can Go in the Composter

Coffee grounds, eggshells, garden refuse that is not diseased, grass clippings, hay, kitchen scraps, leaves, lint from the dryer, peat, straw, tea bags, wood ashes.

Things That Cannot Go in the Composter

Anything inorganic (i.e., metal or plastic), bones, branches or pieces of wood, cat and dog waste, dairy products, diseased plants, meat and fat scraps.

Try not to add too much of any one material at a time; an imbalance can cause a severe reduction in decomposition. Add some fertile soil to each layer to hasten the rotting, and moisten the pile each time you add material. The greater the diversity of materials, the greater the diversity of nutrients that will be available for plants. Bonemeal can be used as an activator, helping to speed decomposition.

Mulching

Mulching simply means covering the soil surface around plants with a foreign material. Here are some good reasons to use a mulch:

- Mulches help the soil to retain moisture, meaning that you will need to water less.
- Mulches help to keep down weeds, by shading them out.
- Many mulches decompose over the summer, adding valuable organic matter to the soil.
- Soil compaction is reduced; walking on a mulch instead of directly on the soil is less likely to pack down the soil.
- Erosion of the soil during heavy rain is lessened.
- The occurrence of soil-inhabiting plant diseases infecting foliage diminishes when soil is prevented from splashing onto leaves (which can transfer disease from the soil to the plant).

Organic mulches, such as peat moss or straw, are best, although you can also use heavy plastic sheeting. Plastic, however, does not decompose, prevent soil compaction, nor eliminate soil erosion. Clear plastic sheeting is not as effective as other mulches for weed control. The best time to apply a mulch is in the spring, after planting.

PREPARING THE SOIL

Soil should be *worked* in the spring to provide a smooth, lump-free seedbed that encourages rapid, even germination of seeds. It is easiest to add organic matter at this time, before tilling, so that it can be worked well into the soil. Dig the organic matter at least 6 inches (15 cm) deep. Turn the soil over with a shovel or spade, break up lumps and remove large rocks.

Using a rototiller can make this less of a chore. Never rototill too finely. Fine soil compacts and crusts easily and is more likely to be washed away by rain. There are models of rototillers designed for use in even very small gardens. After the ground has been thoroughly dug, rake it smooth in preparation for seeding.

If possible, dig the soil again in the fall, leaving large clumps of upturned earth. This rough digging allows freezing and thawing to penetrate the soil clumps and improve soil structure, and kill some overwintering insect pests.

SEEDING

In the relatively short growing season of most Canadian gardens, it makes sense to consider ways to extend it. You can try starting seeds indoors, either in a home greenhouse or under grow lights, using protective covers over crops that are planted early in the spring, and experimenting with seeding in the late fall.

STARTING SEEDS INDOORS

- Fill a seedling flat to within 1/2 an inch (1 cm) of the top edge with a good quality seedling mixture. This is a potting soil with a high percentage of peat moss and perlite. Avoid using garden soil because it tends to become hard, and inhibits proper rooting of the seedlings. Garden soil may also contain insects and diseases.
- As a general rule, sow no deeper than the thickness of the seed.
- Cover with a thin layer of vermiculite, to prevent drying.
- Moisten the soil. Never allow the seedling mix to become dry. Germinating seeds are very intolerant of dry soil and will often die if the soil becomes dry for even a short period of time.
- To get the best possible germination, use a fungicide to prevent "damping off" (rotting of seedlings) shortly after planting the seeds.

Vegetable seeds come in a wide array of sizes and shapes.

- Tag each container with the date planted and variety of seed.
- Cover the flat with a plastic sheet to reduce moisture loss. Use grow lights to enhance germination and growth.
- Place the flat on a heated table, heat register or on top of a refrigerator, to warm the soil and promote rapid germination.
- When the seedlings produce their first set of leaves, fertilize with a plant-starter fertilizer, such as 10-52-10, at one-quarter strength, once a week.
- Use a very fine misting nozzle or misting bottle when watering, to prevent dislodging the seeds in the germination flats.

In order to grow top-quality plants from seed indoors, you will need: seeds, potting soil, seedling trays, fertilizer, grow lights, vermiculite, disease control products, watering equipment.

- Some rapid-growing vegetables, such as tomatoes, peppers and cabbage, should be transplanted into larger containers prior to being transplanted outside. Transplant from seedling flats to larger containers once the first true leaves appear.

Seeding Periods

Vegetables vary greatly in their times from seeding to maturity. This chart helps to determine approximately how long to allow from seeding to transplanting into the garden, for various vegetables. The number of weeks indicated are prior to the date of the average last spring frost.

9-10 weeks (late February-early March)	7-8 weeks (mid-March)	2-4 weeks (early-April)	0-2 weeks (late April-early May)
Celeriac	Eggplants	Broccoli	Cucumbers
Celery	Leeks	Brussels sprouts	Melons
Peppers	Onions	Cabbage	Pumpkins
	Tomatoes	Cauliflower	Squash
		Lettuce	

TRANSPLANTS

Once seedlings have two true leaves, they are generally ready to be transplanted:
- Mark straight rows with string and stakes.
- Dig the planting holes. Transplant at the same depth or just slightly deeper than the plants were growing in their original containers.
- Gently place the transplants into the holes, and firm the soil.
- Water and fertilize immediately. Use a water-soluble *plant starter* fertilizer such as 10-52-10 once a week for the first three weeks after transplanting, to help the root system become established.

Try one of these methods to make small seeds easier to sow:
- mix the seed with some dry sand;
- dribble seed off the end of a trowel;
- use a small seeder (a tool designed for sowing seed).

Saving Seed

If you like to save seed from your crop for sowing the next season, be sure not to save seed of hybrid varieties. The best qualities of a hybrid plant usually exist only in the first generation. Seed collected from a hybrid plant is likely to produce a different plant that is of poor quality.

Treated Seed

Treated seed is lightly coated with a fungicide to protect the seeds and seedlings from *damping off* or rotting. Damping off is a fungal disease that causes seed to rot and kills emerging seedlings. Some treated seed is also coated with an insecticide such as diazinon that protects against root maggots. If the seed has been treated, the packet will say so, and the seed is visibly coated with a coloured powder.

PROTECTING EARLY CROPS

Gamble on reaping an earlier harvest by seeding some vegetables early in the season. I always take a chance by seeding a short row of bush beans in the first part of May, and have been rewarded with an early crop seven years out of ten.

If you plant early, you must provide the plants with protection against frost or cold temperatures. If there is a risk of frost, cover plants with old sheets, blankets, towels, burlap or even a cardboard box. Never cover with plastic; plastic holds cold air and will cause more harm than leaving plants unprotected.

An Earthway ™ seeder is light-weight, easy to use and covers the seed with soil after sowing perfect rows.

You can also protect early crops with materials that are especially designed for this purpose, and that are left in place well into the growing season:

Row Covers: lightweight, durable, spun-bonded polyester fabric available in various lengths and widths, for placing over rows of plants. Captures warmth, insulates from wind, protects from light frosts. Also acts as a barrier to insects. Porous to water, light and air.

Hot Caps: clear plastic forms which are placed over individual plants. Helps to retain warmth, and insulates from light frosts. Hot caps can be purchased, or you can make your own by cutting the tops off large, clear plastic bottles, and poking ventilation holes around the bottoms. Place the inverted bottles over the plants.

PLANTING IN FALL

Experiment with a fall seeding, in late October. Prepare the ground well before seeding, and sow twice as thickly and twice as deep as

Floating row covers over a cucumber crop.

usual, since germination will be less than if seeded in spring. You will have vegetables ready for eating two to four weeks earlier than a spring-planted crop.

Fall-seeding will be successful only in regions where the ground remains frozen from early through late winter.

Vegetables that can be sown in the fall include carrots, lettuce (both leaf and head), onions, parsnips, spinach and Swiss chard.

WATERING

Vegetables need a good, steady supply of moisture, especially when the plants are growing rapidly. Quality is reduced if water is lacking for even a short time. For optimum growth, vegetables should never be allowed to dry out.

Plants in hot, dry areas lose more moisture than those in cooler, more humid areas. As a general rule, vegetables need about 1 inch (2.5 cm) of water per week from rain or irrigation in order to grow vigorously. For example, in a 10-foot by 10-foot (9 m²) garden, 1 inch (2.5 cm) of water would be equal to 50 gallons (227 L) of water.

A simple way to determine how long it would take to apply 1 inch (2.5 cm) of water over this area would be to place the hose, with the nozzle attached, into a 5-gallon (23 L) bucket and open the valve to the setting that you normally use for watering. Time how long it takes to fill the bucket, and multiply this value by ten to determine the amount of time required to provide 1 inch (2.5 cm) of water to the area. Adjust these measurements according to your garden.

Hot, dry days combined with a lack of fertilizer can cause bitterness in vegetables. Inconsistent watering — repeatedly allowing the plants to dry out before watering — often causes further problems, such as splitting of carrots and blossom-end rot in peppers or tomatoes.

Adequate watering is of utmost importance from the time seeds are sown until a couple of weeks after seedlings emergence. Sprouts will have a difficult time pushing through dry, crusted soil. The older the plants become, the more time must be spent watering.

Water wand.

Be patient when watering. Try to water thoroughly, wait for a few minutes for it to soak through, and then water again. Be prepared to water some areas of the garden, especially containers, once or even twice a day in hot weather. There are lots of ways to make watering less of a chore. My favourite method is to use a water wand with a *soft-rain* attachment and shut-off valve, connected to the hose. This attachment is excellent because it provides a large volume of water without damaging plants or dislodging soil. Some models even have a built-in fertilizer dispenser.

Irrigation

Irrigation sprinklers can be used in place of water wands if your garden is very large. Sprinklers that provide a coarse spray of water are suitable for established crops but should not be used on young vegetables, because they tend to compact the soil and can damage new growth. Buying a quality sprinkler will save you money in the long run because it is very durable and more efficient in water usage.
Ask staff at your garden centre for advice.
Reduce excessive water evaporation losses by watering in the morning or evening, and avoid watering on windy days.

FERTILIZING

Plants require three major nutrients in relatively large quantities: nitrogen, phosphorous and potassium. Even rich soils rarely contain an optimum supply for all vegetables. It is usually necessary to supplement.

The three numbers on fertilizer containers indicate the percentage of major nutrients by weight. For example, a 10-52-10 fertilizer contains a minimum of 10 % nitrogen, 52 % phosphate (phosphorus) and 10 % potash (potassium).

Nitrogen (N): promotes leafy plant growth and lush leaves. Important for these vegetables: Cabbage, Corn, Cucumbers. Good organic sources: blood meal, sheep manure.

Phosphorous (P): promotes root development, flower production, increased fruit set and earlier ripening. Important for these vegetables: Corn, Onions, Potatoes. Good organic sources: bonemeal, rock phosphate, dolomitic lime.

Potassium (K): fruit quality and disease resistance. Important for these vegetables: Celery, Cucumbers, Tomatoes. Good organic sources: kelp meal, sheep manure.

PEST CONTROL

Weeds

Weeds compete with vegetables for space, water, nutrients and sunlight, and can substantially reduce the harvest. The best time to control weeds is at the seedling stage, long before they become established.

Perennial weeds such as thistle and quack grass must be controlled prior to planting vegetables. Areas of the garden that contain perennial weeds should not be planted until the weeds have been eliminated.

For control of annual weeds, try this simple method. A week after planting, take a rake, point the prongs at the sky, and very lightly stir the soil where you have just seeded. Many germinating weed seeds will be exposed to the air and die; most vegetable seeds are deep enough not to be affected by raking.

Pigs in the Garden

One year our 12 sows got into the garden and rolled around in the soft soil where we had just seeded. I was just sick about it. I figured they had ruined our carrot patch. We had rain, and about a week later, I went out to the garden, looked down and saw perfect rows of carrots, all along where the pigs had rolled. Wherever they had rolled, they were no weeds — other areas were extremely weedy. I told this story years later at one of my gardening talks, and one of the guests said that was called *stirring the soil*. She has done it in her gardens ever since she was a little girl, over about 60 years of gardening. It was amazing to hear this wonderful lady describe practising for years what we had discovered by accident: stirring the soil.

"In the spring when seeds are sprouting,
stir the land.
In the summer, nothing doubting,
stir the land.
Stirring helps each little seed,
stirring kills each little weed,
stirring; let this be your creed:
stir the land."

Mrs. C. Lauman, *A Farm Woman from Alberta*

Disease & Insects

There are many methods of pest control but the most important one is prevention. Many problems can be avoided by simply keeping the garden clean and the plants in the healthiest possible state. Insects prefer plants that are weak or stressed. Healthy plants, however, are not immune to attack, just less prone.

Keeping the garden clean involves removing all crop remains once the harvest has been completed, and promptly disposing of any diseased or insect-infested plants. This is especially important in the fall, when insects are searching for places to lay eggs or to hibernate. Turning the soil will expose eggs and grubs to birds and freezing temperatures.

Control cabbage worms by handpicking, or with an application of BT or rotenone.

Some crops, such as cucumbers and melons, are prone to soilborne diseases, which can be transferred from the soil to the leaves by splashing rain. Mulching around these plants before the vines spread provides a protective *splash barrier*. Other diseases can be avoided by staying away from vegetables such as beans, cucumbers and melons whenever the plants are wet.

Experiment by including in your vegetable garden those plants which are reputed to have pest-repellent qualities: chrysanthemums, marigolds, and chives, for example, and several herbs. Be aware of and encourage beneficial insects, such as ladybugs and lacewings, which feed on *bad bugs* such as aphids that destroy plants. Choose disease-resistant varieties of vegetables, especially if you are consistently having a disease problem.

If you do run into a pest problem, consider the options. If the infestation is slight, you may be able to remove the affected portion, or perhaps just one or two plants. Always be prepared to tolerate some losses from pests. Fighting off insects and diseases can sometimes involve a lot of effort. It might be preferable to re-seed or transplant a second crop if the problem occurs early enough in the season.

If the problem is more than can be easily controlled by manual means, and you want to apply a pesticide, be aware that an *organic* label does not guarantee that the product is necessarily any safer or controls any better than a *chemical* pesticide. Be cautious when applying any pesticide, always fully read the instructions, and get advice from professionals prior to application.

Here are some of the common *organic* insecticides:

Bacillus thuringiensis (BT): a commercially-packaged bacteria which is particularly effective against caterpillars, cabbage worms and loopers. BT degrades quickly after application and must be reapplied after a rainfall. It is not harmful to plants, animals, humans or beneficial insects, and can be used up to the day of harvest. It is most effective when applied on young insects. Very safe.

Diatomaceous earth: made from the pulverized remains of tiny fossilized ocean organisms called diatoms. Diatomaceous earth is very effective on soft-bellied insects and slugs, and kills on contact by removing the pests' protective outer coating, causing them to dry up. It is effective on a wide range of insects, including aphids and caterpillars. Reapply after a rainfall. Diatomaceous earth will not harm earthworms, animals or humans. Safe.

Insecticidal soap: a soap specifically formulated to kill insects through suffocation and disruption of fine membranes. Aphids, mites, leafhoppers and whiteflies are some of the insects that it controls, but they must be thoroughly coated for it to be effective. Insecticidal soap biodegrades quickly and must be reapplied after a rainfall. It does not harm most beneficial insects. Very safe.

Pyrethrum: a naturally-occurring insecticide that is derived from chrysanthemum flowers. It is an effective control for aphids, various beetles, caterpillars, thrips and other insects, but it is also toxic to fish, frogs and many beneficial insects. Do not use where spray can drift into lakes or streams, and discontinue use one week before harvest. Use with discretion.

Rotenone: a naturally-occurring insecticide, derived from the roots of tropical plants. It is effective against various caterpillars, flea beetles, leafhoppers, potato bugs and squash beetles, among other insects. Its effectiveness is not long-lasting; dust or spray carefully on a calm evening.

Chemical pesticides can be very safe and effective when used properly. If you prefer to use a chemical pest control, take a sample of the affected plant into your local garden centre, to ensure that you have correctly identified the problem. Ask staff for advice on recommended methods of treatment, and be sure to carefully read the instructions on the label before using any pesticide.

STORAGE

The home gardener rarely has ideal vegetable storage conditions, however, the closer one can get to providing the best storage environment for each vegetable, the longer they will last.

Storage Hints

Do not store root crops with apples, pears or other fruits, including tomatoes. These fruits give off ethylene gas which causes deterioration of most vegetables. As a general rule, it is best to harvest vegetables on a cool, dry day. Vegetables harvested when temperatures are hot will not last as long in storage.

For information on storage and recommended conditions see the chart in Appendix I on page 155.

SPECIALTY VEGETABLE GARDENS

SPECIALTY SALAD GARDENING

I have always admired the French for their high vegetable-quality standards and their ingenuity in growing. In southern France, it is common to plant an entire salad in one area of a garden, and to harvest the mixture for a *salade de mesclun*. Mesclun salads are simply comprised of leafy vegetables and are grown as they are served, without adding anything other than dressing, and perhaps a few edible flowers for additional zest and colour. Mesclun has a wonderful array of tastes, colours and textures, because of the variety of greens, which are customized to suit the preferences of the individual gardener.

The skill is in choosing a mixture of greens with visual appeal and complimentary flavour, which matures at roughly the same time. The fun is in experimenting with different combinations for the perfect pre-mixed salad. The beauty is in the simplicity.

Plants that are suitable for mesclun include various types of leaf lettuce, and any other leafy vegetables or herbs that you care to try. The more colourful the leaf lettuce, the better. Push a few scallions at random into the patch; the pungent greens of these onions add a spicy accent to salads.

Plant mesclun in a container to prevent unwanted weeds joining in the mix. Simply combine the mesclun seed and broadcast it onto the soil. The greens grow closely together and are harvested young, when only a few inches (5 to 7.5 cm) high, by snipping with scissors across the salad patch. Keep a close eye on moisture levels; you may need to water daily during hot weather.

Mesclun Ingredients

Mesclun salads can be simply comprised of two or three types of leaf lettuces, or can include a wide array of salad greens and herbs (my favourites include basil, and various types of mint and parsley). Here are some suggestions to experiment with, in small amounts, for more diversity:

Early Crops
Chervil, Chicory, Spinach
Mild Flavour
Corn Salad (mache), Purslane
Tart Flavour
Chicory, Endive
Spicy Flavour
Arugula, Cress, Mustard greens
Zest
Basil, Coriander, Dill, Fennel,
Mint, Oregano, Parsley, Sorrel

Edible Blossoms
Colour & Delicate Flavour
Calendula, Cowslips, Johnny -
Jump-Ups, Pansy, Tagetes
Mildly Spicy
Chive blossoms, Nasturtiums
Other
Monarda (lemony-mint flavour)

CONTAINER GARDENS

Many vegetables can be grown in large patio containers, with remarkable results. On a sunny balcony or deck, it is possible to cultivate a pleasing assortment, and to reap a considerable harvest. Keep in mind, however, that container-grown vegetables require extra watering and fertilizing for the best yields.

Almost any type of container will do, provided that it is fairly large. I have even planted cucumbers in some old five-gallon (22 L) black plastic buckets, and harvested both pickling and slicing varieties much earlier in the season than the garden-grown cucumbers.

For a more ornamental display, choose an attractive container, and plant some flowers along with the vegetables. Lobelia adds bright colour and alyssum adds fragrance; both grow well in containers. Nasturtiums have edible flowers, and tagetes marigolds are reputed to repel insects. Sweet peas grown with runner beans make a lovely, scented pillar, and basil, with its fragrant, spicy leaves, can be added to a hanging basket of tomatoes. Almost any type of herb can be included in the pots.

Container gardening — cucumbers growing vertically in five-gallon buckets.

Be prepared to water container gardens every day in hot weather. Hanging baskets dry out more quickly than other types of containers. To ensure that roots have received adequate moisture, I like to soak the plants until the water runs from the bottom of the pots. If, however, the soil has become so dry that it has pulled away from the edges of the container, you will need to soak the soil repeatedly to ensure that water is reaching the roots of the plants, and not just running down the inside edges of the container.

Regular fertilizing is particularly important with container gardens. The original soil nutrients are soon used up through constant watering and by the requirements of the large number of plants in a small space. Fertilize most containers once a week; for hanging baskets of tomatoes or cucumbers, add a pinch of fertilizer to the watering can each time you water.

Vegetables that Grow Well in Containers

Beans, Cucumbers, Eggplant, Garlic, Lettuce (leaf), Melons, Peppers, Spinach, Squash, Tomatoes.

GARDENING IN SMALL SPACES

Intensive gardening is the practice of growing a large number of different plants closely together in a small area, for the purpose of producing more food from less space. Here are various methods of intensive gardening:

Raised Beds

In the *French Intensive* method of gardening, vegetables or other types of plants are grown in raised beds, with orderly pathways running in between.

Raised beds are filled with a light peat moss/soil mixture that has several advantages over garden soil: drainage is superior, the soil mixture warms quickly in the spring, resulting in earlier-maturing crops, and it contains fewer weeds.

For the handicapped or elderly gardener, the beds can be raised to a height which is accessible from a wheelchair or seated position, and designed so that all areas are within an arm's reach, from either side of the garden bed.

Square Foot Gardening

Square foot gardening is an orderly and effective method of planting in small spaces. The garden is divided into 4 ft² blocks (1.5 m²), with pathways running between the blocks. Each one foot (30 cm) square within the block is planted with a specific number of plants. For example, a single block may contain one tomato or pepper plant, two cucumber plants, or eight plants of peas or beans.

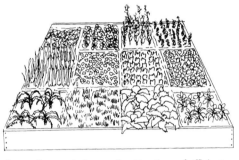

Square foot gardening can be attractive and efficient.

I have never tried square foot gardening myself, but know a man who has used this method for the past few years with great success. His garden is stunning — very neat and attractive, and packed full of vegetables of every description.

Square foot gardening is a low-maintenance method of growing vegetables, that attempts to closely match production with consumption, thus avoiding wastage of food and space. For more information on this method of growing, see the book *Square Foot Gardening*, by Mel Bartholomew.

Vertical Gardening

Vertical gardening is the practice of growing vining or climbing plants on a trellis or other support, rather than allowing them to sprawl horizontally along the ground. This can involve cucumbers or pole beans running up fences, sprawling squash or melon vines loosely tied to a *wigwam* or *teepee* of poles, or tomatoes caged, staked or attached to a frame of strings.

Vertically-grown crops hold their fruit well off the ground, which means the vegetables are cleaner and there is less chance of rotting or soil-borne diseases being transferred to the plants. Air circulation is improved, which reduces the incidence of a disease such as mildew. I have found that when my peas were planted in an area with good air circulation, I had no problem with mildew, but did the next year, when I planted peas in an area where the air circulation was poorer.

Vertically-grown crops are also easy to pick, and have maximum exposure to sunlight, which can result in increased production. Almost any vegetable or flower that produces a vine can be grown vertically.

VEGETABLE GARDENS FOR CHILDREN

If you have children, consider giving them a small area of the garden to grow vegetables. Gardening can be an educational experience that also provides children with a sense of accomplishment. It can be fun too — most kids love digging around in the dirt and will enjoy watching the plants grow. You may also be surprised at how much easier it is to get children to eat vegetables from their own garden, than to eat them at the dinner table.

Most children love gardening, but can be restless and impatient. Try to make it fun, rather than a chore. Keep the area small enough to be fairly manageable for a child, plant vegetables that are quick and easy to grow, and expect to help out at times.

Choose mainly those vegetables which have seeds large enough to be easily handled by little hands.

These proud young gardeners can't wait to plant their tomato seedlings.

Consider starting seeds indoors, so the children can see them begin to sprout. Let the children dig the garden and sow the seeds, and allow them the responsibility of watering the plants during the season. Tending the plants through to maturity can be a rewarding and satisfying experience that provides children with a sense of accomplishment, especially when they can eat the fruits of their labour.

Recommended Vegetables
for Children's Gardens

Beans, Carrots, Kohlrabi, Peas, Pumpkins, Sunflowers, Tomatoes.

ASPARAGUS

Asparagus differs from most vegetables in that it produces a harvestable crop very early in the spring. The bare young spears poke through the earth, providing a striking contrast against stark black soil. Tall, attractive ferns with bright red berries are produced later. Asparagus grows best in cool, northern climates.

RECOMMENDED VARIETIES

Martha Washington (Mary Washington) • hardy; high yields; resistant to the asparagus rust disease. (White asparagus spears can be produced by simply covering the growing shoots with mounded soil, as you would hill potatoes. Harvest when spear tips poke through the earth.)

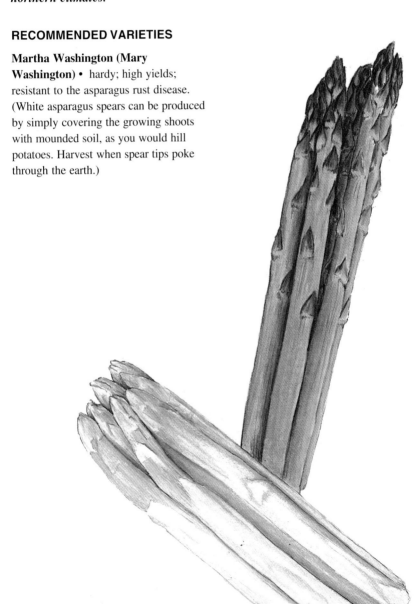

BEFORE YOU PLANT

• Clear the area of all vegetation. Keeping weeds at bay will extend the life of your asparagus bed. Do not plant other perennials nearby.

• Cultivate the soil as deeply as possible and work in a generous amount of composted manure. Asparagus needs a good supply of phosphorus, so add one handful of bonemeal per plant before planting and work it lightly into the soil.

WHEN TO PLANT

• Plant in early spring. Strong crowns with at least ten roots are best. I prefer two-year-old crowns, because you can harvest some spears the year after planting, but if these are not available, plant one-year-old crowns. Remember, though, to take only a limited harvest from one-year-old crowns for the first year after planting. Starting asparagus from seed is not recommended, because it will be three to four years before a crop can be harvested.

HOW MUCH TO PLANT

• Each plant will yield half a dozen or more spears during the harvest period. Expect a limited harvest in the first season from one-year-old crowns, but to reap more each following year.

• An established bed will last from 15 to 20 years, and even longer if weeds are kept under control.

One cup (250 ml) of cooked asparagus provides two-thirds of the daily recommended allowance of vitamin C, one-third the daily recommended allowance of vitamin A.

PLANTING METHODS

• Dig a trench 6 inches (15 cm) deep; spread roots apart and cover with not more than 2 inches (5 cm) of well-firmed soil. During the second season as the plants grow, gradually fill in the trench until it is level with the garden.

• If in a row, space plants every 12 inches (30 cm) along trenches that are 4 feet (120 cm) apart.

• If in a bed, allow 2 feet (60 cm) between plants.

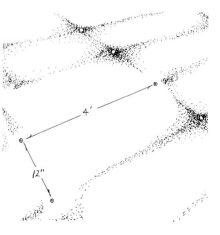

4'

12"

GROWING TIPS

- Feed new plants with a "starter" fertilizer, such as 10-52-10, once a week for the first three weeks after transplanting, to help establish a strong root system.

- Keeping the asparagus bed free of weeds throughout each growing season will add years to its life.

- Remember to give asparagus a heavy watering in October. You will be rewarded by an earlier crop the following spring.

Try eating asparagus raw: the taste is surprisingly similar to that of fresh garden peas. Serve whole stalks with a vegetable dip, or chop them into a salad.

HARVESTING

- Harvesting may be started in the year following planting; do not pick any spears in the year that you plant.

- Excessive harvesting in any season may reduce your yield the following year. If this happens, cut spears over a shorter period, and allow the plant to build up its reserves. The result will be a vigourous growth of spears the next year.

- In the first harvest year, cut only for two to three weeks. In the second cutting year, harvest for three to four weeks, and in the following seasons, from four to six weeks.

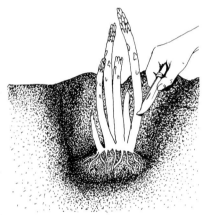

Cut spears just below ground level.

- Harvest only for the recommended period: you must allow some spears to produce mature leaves so that the plant can establish reserves for next year's crop.

- Judge readiness by width rather than height. Stalks the thickness of a finger are tastier than thinner ones.

- Pick spears every other day, or even daily, to get the best yield.

- The best time to harvest is in the morning, or about half an hour before you are ready to cook. Avoid harvesting at mid-day.

- Twist or cut stalks with a sharp knife, just below ground level. If stalks do not cut easily, they are likely over-mature. Take care not to damage young spears which have not yet poked through the ground.

- Never cut the ferns after harvesting; allow them to die back on their own in the fall. Ferns should be left standing over the winter to trap snow around the plants, providing moisture and insulating the roots from cold. Ferns can be removed in the spring.

STORAGE

• Fresh asparagus is very perishable and loses quality rapidly. Collect the spears as soon as possible, protect them from the sun and move to cold storage as soon as possible. Store asparagus unwashed in the refrigerator, and clean it just before you are ready to cook.

Experiment with these herbs when using asparagus in the kitchen: chives, lemon balm, sage, savory, tarragon, thyme.

PROBLEMS

What are common problems with growing asparagus?

Asparagus is relatively pest-free because it is ready early in the season, prior to the appearance of most insects and disease. Rust disease is one problem that occurs, but it can be avoided by planting resistant varieties. Keeping the planting bed clean during the growing season will prevent most other problems.

Steamed Asparagus with Lemon & Butter

A simple & nutritious dish with the tang of lemon.

Fresh, young garden asparagus is so tender that the entire stalk can be eaten. Wash spears and lay in a pan. Steam lightly. Drain, add butter and lemon to taste, and season with freshly cracked pepper, if desired. Serve immediately.

Asparagus is ready for harvest when the spears are as thick as your forefinger.

BEANS

Determining bean types can be confusing: string beans are also known as French beans, snap beans and bush beans; pole beans can be string or runner beans; broad beans are also called faba, English or Italian beans. I find it simplest to categorize them by their growth habits — simply as bush or pole beans. Broad beans are in a class of their own.

RECOMMENDED VARIETIES

Bush

Bush Romano • green, stringless, Italian-type beans; matures mid-season.

Greencrop • flat green pods so long they often touch the ground; matures early.

Peak • very slim, green, stringless beans; a gourmet variety; matures mid-season.

Rocdor • an extra-tasty yellow (wax) bean; matures early.

Royal Burgundy • striking, flavourful purple pods, which turn green when cooked; matures mid-season.

Strike • long, slim, tender green beans; high yields; matures early.

Pole

Scarlet Runner • tender green beans; beautiful, bright red flowers; makes a stunning display growing in a half-barrel planter; pick very young pods and beans to eat like string beans, and later use as green shell beans; matures late season.

Broad

Broad Windsor Long Pod • long pods; matures late season.

Toto • dwarf plant; matures late season.

Rocdor

Royal Burgundy

Strike

Toto

BEFORE YOU PLANT

• Inoculants are naturally-occurring materials that contain soil bacteria. They help bean plants extract nitrogen (a nutrient that is essential to growth) from the soil. Simply mix this dry, sooty powder with your seed before planting. Use a thick coating to increase yields. Buy inoculant fresh each year, and avoid exposing it to heat and sunlight. Excess inoculant can be worked into the soil.

• Few vegetable seeds decay more quickly in cold, wet soil than beans. For early plantings, use "treated" seed, which is coated with a mild fungicide to prevent the seeds from rotting. If you are planting early into cool soil, and prefer not to use treated seed, sow more thickly, as some seed is likely to rot.

• Some people soak seeds before planting to speed germination. I think soaking seed is unnecessary, and can create problems. Tender sprouts will die if allowed to dry out. Uncooperative weather can create several problems: too dry, and you will need to water daily to keep seeds alive; too wet, and you will be unable to get into the garden to plant the already sprouted seed. Instead of soaking seed, I simply plant into warm, moist soil.

• Try to choose a site where beans or peas have not been planted for at least a year. Rotating crops will reduce the incidence of insect and disease problems.

One-half cup (125 ml) of cooked beans provides one-third the daily recommended allowance of vitamin A.

WHEN TO PLANT

• If possible, sow beans three times: in late May, early June and again in mid-June. This ensures a steady supply of tender beans during the harvest season.

• I always take a chance by seeding a short row in the first part of May, and have been rewarded with an early crop seven years out of ten.

• Bush and pole beans can be planted in the first week of May but you must use treated seed. Cover young seedlings with an old blanket if there is a risk of frost. I always sow thicker than many experts recommend, to ensure a good stand even if some plants are destroyed by frost or pests.

• Only broad beans can withstand a light frost and cool soil temperatures: sow them from the end of April to the end of May. Broad beans take longer to mature than the other types. A late second planting gives you a crop throughout the summer; however, these beans age more quickly in hot weather.

HOW MUCH TO PLANT

Bush beans: In a small garden, sow only a single row at a time. One 10-foot (3 m) row will yield about 8 pounds (3.5 kg) of beans; yellow varieties yield slightly less.

Pole beans: Most pole varieties mature later than bush beans, but produce more — about 12 pounds (5.5 kg) per 10-foot (3 m) row.

Broad beans: Most varieties produce about 10 pounds (4.5 kg) per 10-foot (3 m) row.

PLANTING METHODS

• Sow seeds to the depth of your second knuckle. Sow broad beans slightly deeper, because the seed is larger.

Bush: Plant a single row, with seeds 1 - 1 1/2 inches (2.5 - 3.5 cm) apart.

Pole: Plant five to six seeds around each pole.

Broad: Plant single or double rows, with 1 inch (2.5 cm) between seeds and 8 inches (20 cm) between rows.

Colourful Beans

• Try planting different cultivars of bush beans within the row — purple, yellow and green — for a colourful display in the garden and variety on the table. For best results, choose varieties which will mature at approximately the same time.

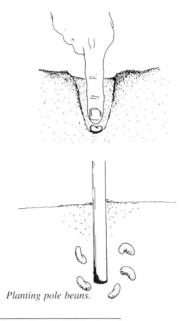

Planting pole beans.

Experiment with these herbs when using beans in the kitchen: basil, caraway, cloves, dill, marjoram, mint, sage, savory, thyme.

GROWING TIPS

• I no longer stake my bush beans; the varieties I like stand high off the soil without support. Greencrop, however, often has pods so long that they touch the ground; pick those pods right away as they will rot if allowed to lay on damp soil. Remember to be gentle with the plants when harvesting so as not to break the stems.

• Pole beans need a support to climb on; use poles, strings, trellises or make a tee-pee, as high as you care to pick. Pole beans will climb as high as you let them. They are most manageable if you stake them to a height that is easy to reach, and then simply train the vines to climb back down.

• Broad bean plants do not need to be staked.

• Adequate watering is most important during and immediately after flowering, and once pods have formed, in order for the plants to produce a high yield of evenly-shaped beans.

• Never weed or work in your bean patch when the plants are the least bit damp. Following this simple rule will reduce the spread of disease.

• Avoid tilling plants too closely, as most of the bean plant's roots are in the top 8 inches (20 cm) of soil.

HARVESTING

- Pick beans when the pods are still young and tender.

- Begin to harvest broad beans when pods are 2 to 3 inches (5 - 7.5 cm) long, and cook them whole. Pick for shelling when the shape of the beans begins to show through the pod, but before the bean's "smile" turns dark — it should still be white or green.

- Harvest often to increase yield, and remove all mature pods, even those too old for eating. Old pods rob the younger, developing pods of nutrients and reduce the yield of high quality, tender beans.

- Beans taste best fresh from the garden; at each harvest, I usually pick only what I need for the next meal.

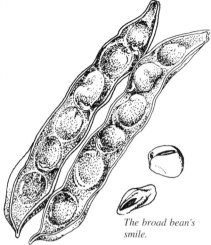

The broad bean's smile.

- The roots of bean plants contain a lot of nitrogen and will enrich the soil. Till finished plants under or add them to your compost heap. This practice also helps to control pests. Be sure to put any bug-infested or diseased plants into the garbage. "Heavy-feeding" vegetables (those which require a lot of nutrients) such as corn, celery and potatoes, are good choices to follow beans in crop rotation.

STORAGE

- Store string beans inside plastic bags in the refrigerator. They will remain fresh for a week or longer. Do not wash or cut ends off beans until you are ready to use them.

PROBLEMS

My bean plants have rust-coloured patches on their leaves. What is wrong?

This is probably a rust fungus, that lives over winters on the remains of diseased plants. Pull up and destroy affected plants to prevent it from spreading. To reduce rust problems, keep your garden clean, plant resistant varieties, and avoid working in your bean patch when the plants are wet.

What causes the dark streaks on my beans?

Some diseases cause streaking, although it could just be the natural appearance of the variety. I once had a man show me some beans that he thought were diseased because the pods were streaked with purple. He was extremely relieved when I told him that what he had was simply a gourmet variety that is often used in French cuisine — a French Filet bush bean. The Marbel variety is a good example of this. Its colour changes to an appetizing bright green once the beans are cooked.

BEETS

Beets (beetroots) are one of the vegetables that I depend upon for visual appeal on the dinner table: rich red beets served with a nice green vegetable are wonderful against the bland hues of meat and potatoes. For this reason I rarely grow the yellow and white varieties, although their taste is lovely. I like to cook beets and greens in the same pot; start out with just the beetroots and in the last few minutes, lay the greens over top to steam lightly.

RECOMMENDED VARIETIES

Albino White • sweet, round, creamy-white beets; roots do not "bleed"; tasty greens; matures early.

Burpee's Golden • tender, round, golden beets; roots do not "bleed"; tasty greens; matures early.

Formanova • cylindrical, red roots slice evenly into perfect pickles; matures early to mid-season.

Little Egypt • round, red beets; the earliest variety available.

Red Ace • unusual honey-sweet flavour; round, red beets; the best variety for pickling; resists bolting; matures early.

Formanova

Little Egypt

BEFORE YOU PLANT

• Work the soil well and remove clumps and stones so roots can develop quickly and uniformly. Add compost and well-rotted manure; avoid fresh manure as roots will become hairy.

WHEN TO PLANT

• Seed beets at least twice, with about two weeks between plantings. You can usually sow them in late April, as soon as the ground has thawed and can be worked.

• Sow your main crop in the last two weeks of May or early in June.

HOW MUCH TO PLANT

• Expect to harvest about 10 pounds (4.5 kg) of beets from a 10-foot (3 m) row.

• If you prefer small beets for eating, double the amount of seed. Crowding keeps the roots small; the more room they are given, the larger they will grow.

• I always seed Little Egypt first and two crops of Red Ace, one early and the second two to three weeks later. The Little Egypt crop will be consumed before the first seeding of Red Ace matures, and the delay between sowings allows time to use up those beets before the final crop matures.

PLANTING METHODS

• Sow seeds to the depth of the fingernail of your index finger.

• Sprinkle seeds along double or triple rows spaced 3 inches (7.5 cm) apart.

Earliest Harvest

• Sow a single row of Little Egypt for the earliest crop. These beets will be ready for eating about two weeks sooner than all other varieties. I never plant a lot of this variety since its roots quickly become tough and woody, but when eaten just when the roots reach the size of a golf ball or slightly smaller, these beets are delicious.

Meadow Seeding

• Scatter your seed in a 1-foot-wide (30 cm) band to create a miniature meadow of beets. This method works very well in a small garden.

Beautiful Beets

• All types of beets will grow well together. Plant a mixed crop of red, yellow and white beets, and create delectable dishes and pretty pickles with a variety of flavours and colours. Some seed companies sell packets of mixed seed, but it is just as easy to blend your own.

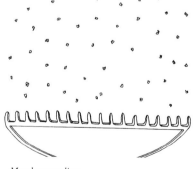

Meadow seeding.

GROWING TIPS

• Try this simple method to reduce future weeding: about a week after sowing, take a rake, point the prongs at the sky, and very lightly stir the soil where you have just seeded. Germinating weed seeds will be exposed to the air and die; the vegetable seeds have not yet germinated and will be fine.

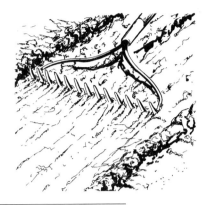

Beets are high in vitamins A, C and iron. The greens are higher in vitamins than the roots.

HARVESTING

• Young beet greens are superb! Cook them like spinach and serve with butter and lemon juice or make a marvellous salad. To harvest greens, pick the entire plant when the leaves are 4 to 6 inches (10 - 15 cm) tall — work your way through the row and this will serve as thinning. If you do not care for the greens, give them to a neighbour or friend, and keep the roots — baby beets taste wonderful.

• Harvest beets whenever they reach a size that you like to eat. I find young beets with small, firm roots and crisp green leaves are the most tender and tasty.

• Thin as you harvest by picking your way through the row.

Experiment with these herbs when using beets in the kitchen: chives, cloves, dill, ginger, mint, nutmeg, paprika.

STORAGE

• I often cook more than I need for a meal, and freeze beets right inside a casserole dish. Later, just retrieve the casserole, place a dab of butter on top and warm it in the oven.

• Before storing, twist off the greens 2 inches (5 cm) above the crown; cut tops tend to bleed. Leave tap root end intact.

• Beets last up to six months inside a crock with the lid on, kept in a dark coldroom. In the refrigerator, they keep about one month inside perforated plastic bags. Greens stay fresh for five to six days placed in a plastic bag and refrigerated.

PROBLEMS

My beet leaves are full of tiny, round holes. What could be the cause?

Flea beetles often attack in spring, leaving small "shot" holes and slowing the plant's growth. The beetles are very tiny and jump like fleas when disturbed. At the first sign of damage, apply rotenone (a natural insecticide, derived from the roots of tropical plants), to the foliage.

Pickled Beets

Cook beets until tender. Drain and run under cold water. Cut large beets into pieces; use small beets whole. Pack into sterilized jars.

Prepare brine. For every 3 cups (750 ml) white vinegar, add 3 cups (750 ml) white sugar. Bring brine to rolling boil for approximately 2 minutes. Fill jars with hot brine and seal. For variety, add pickling spice to some jars. For sweeter pickles, add more sugar; for sour pickles, add less.

I always fill a crock as well as the jars, to keep on the counter and scoop out beets as needed. Beet pickles store perfectly in a crock for a couple of weeks.

The greens of Red Ace beets remain tasty, even when the roots are quite large.

BROCCOLI

I was introduced to broccoli many years ago by our Italian customers, at a time when many North American families had never heard of it. It has become one of our staple vegetables, and its bright colour is a welcome addition to the table. Now, many varieties are available for growing: purple-headed and sprouting varieties which turn green when cooked; Romanesco types with unusual, spiralled and peaked, pale green heads; even a yellow-headed hybrid cauliflower-cross. I like to experiment with different varieties, new colours and surprising flavours, but the traditional type remains my favourite.

Broccoli is a member of the Brassica family, along with cabbage, cauliflower, Brussels sprouts, kale and kohlrabi. These plants all require the same care while growing and are attractive to the same pests, although kale and kohlrabi less than the others. It is worthwhile to consider growing them in one section of the garden; that way, if pests strike, you can concentrate your efforts.

RECOMMENDED VARIETIES

Paragon • an early-maturing variety which produces very tender, sweet heads 6 to 8 inches (15 - 20 cm) across, excellent fresh and for freezing.

Premium Crop • matures later, with flat, single heads about 10 inches (25 cm) across.

Goliath • has the largest heads, up to 12 inches (30 cm) wide, and matures early.

BEFORE YOU PLANT

• Try to choose a site where no cabbage-related plants were planted for the last two years, because diseases can build up in the soil.

WHEN TO PLANT

• Broccoli can be seeded outside from April until June. The young plants can withstand light frosts.

• Sow three successive plantings about four weeks apart, or an early and late-maturing variety for a continuous supply. I often plant from the last week of April to the first of May, again from the last week of May to the first of June, and finally in the last week of June to the first of July, with the last crop available for harvest right through the fall.

• For the earliest crop, sow seeds indoors the first week of April and transplant outdoors at the beginning of May. If you are buying plants from a greenhouse, choose small ones. Seedlings which have been growing in a container for more than six weeks will not produce a good crop.

HOW MUCH TO PLANT

• Expect to harvest about 1 3/4 pounds (700 g) per plant.

PLANTING METHODS

• Sow at fingertip depth.

• Plant seeds 1 to 2 inches (2.5 - 5 cm) apart in rows or squares.

• Treat all members of the cabbage family in the same manner. Lay newspaper or tar-paper squares around seedlings to help prevent root maggot damage; insert collars over seedlings to discourage cutworms; and consider companion plantings of chives and garlic, which are reputed to aid in repelling pests.

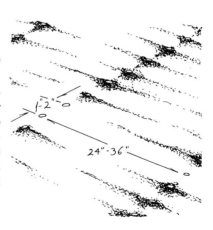

GROWING TIPS

• Allow plants to reach 6 to 10 inches (15 - 25 cm) before thinning, as there is a chance of losing some to insects. Thin to about 6 inches (15 cm) between plants; closely-spaced plants will produce smaller, more tender heads.

Broccoli contains vitamin A, iron and minerals.

HARVESTING

- Pick broccoli during the coolest part of the day, before plants have absorbed the sun's heat. Harvesting in the morning is usually best.

- In warm conditions, even harvested heads will produce tiny yellow flowers. Once I left a basket full of cut broccoli sitting outdoors in the late afternoon; within a few hours, it had all turned yellow.

- Harvest the central head when it is still hard and green, and cut 3 to 4 inches (7.5 - 10 cm) of stem. The plant will develop smaller side shoots, enabling you to harvest over a longer period.

- Broccoli can be harvested at any size. Harvest more often when the weather is warm. Do not let any buds go to flower.

Harvest the central head and the plant will develop side shoots.

Experiment with these herbs when using broccoli in the kitchen: basil, dill, garlic, lemon balm, marjoram, oregano, tarragon, thyme.

STORAGE

- Store broccoli inside a plastic bag in the refrigerator; use within three days.

PROBLEMS

How do I control cabbage worms?

At the first sign of these worms, apply bacillus thuringiensis (BT, a biological control) or rotenone. BT can be used right up to the day of harvest; however, it usually takes three to four days to become effective, and it should be re-applied after a rainfall.

The variety Goliath produces a huge head, up to 12 inches (30 cm) across.

BRUSSELS SPROUTS

Brussels sprouts are an interesting and rewarding vegetable to grow. Although never a sure crop, because they require a long, favourable season, I think they are well worth the time and effort. This vegetable is favoured in Great Britain, and it was at my British mother-in-law's dinner table that I first tasted Brussels sprouts, when I was in my early twenties.

RECOMMENDED VARIETIES

Jade Cross • fairly quick to mature; resistant to diseases; produces a high yield of flavourful sprouts. Most Brussels sprouts are green although there are also red varieties available.

WHEN TO PLANT

- Brussels sprouts need a long growing season. If you are able to get into your garden in the first few weeks of April, attempt to plant a few seeds, sown at fingertip depth, 1 to 2 inches (2.5 - 5 cm) apart in rows or squares. To ensure that some Brussels sprouts mature before an early freeze-up, always transplant at least a few seedlings.

- Transplant in early to mid-May. If you are buying plants from a greenhouse, choose small plants. Seedlings which have been growing in a container for more than six weeks will not produce a good crop.

Experiment with these herbs when using Brussels sprouts in the kitchen: dill, garlic, parsley, tarragon.

HOW MUCH TO PLANT

- Each plant will yield at least 1 pound (500 g) of sprouts.

- One stalk has enough sprouts to serve with a meal for a small family.

PLANTING METHODS

- Transplant just slightly deeper than plants were growing in their containers.

- Set the plants about 6 inches (15 cm) apart in rows or squares.

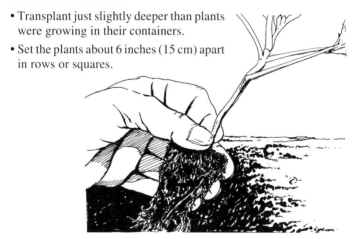

GROWING TIPS

- If you have a direct-seeded crop, thin the plants to about 6 inches (15 cm) apart three weeks after they have emerged from the soil.

- The best-quality sprouts come from plants that are well-watered and fertilized throughout the season. Cool, wet summers are ideal for this vegetable.

- Pinch out the central growing point at the top of plant about mid-September to encourage rapid development of upper sprouts.

HARVESTING

• Twist or snap sprouts off when they become firm and solid. The bottom sprouts mature first. For early sprouts, I usually work my way along the row, taking about six sprouts from each plant until I have enough for a meal.

• Leave plants in the garden for the first light fall frosts, as frost improves the flavour. Cut the entire stalk before the first hard frost, and bring it indoors for storage. Generally I do this soon after the final potato harvest.

Cook Brussels sprouts uncovered to keep them a nice bright green, and take care not to overcook.

STORAGE

• Store single sprouts inside a plastic bag in the refrigerator, and use within five days. Hang a stalk in a cool, dry, dark place; the sprouts will keep for several weeks.

PROBLEMS

Why do my Brussels sprouts plants turn brown, topple over and die, early in the season?

Most likely they have been attacked by root maggots, the larvae of a fly that lays its eggs on the soil near the plants. To prevent root maggot problems, cover the soil with newspaper, as close to the plants as possible. This prevents the parent flies from laying eggs in the soil; if they leave their eggs on the newspaper, the eggs will dry out in the sun and die.

As a general rule, when saskatoon bushes bloom, the adult flies are laying their eggs. This is the best time to achieve control. All members of the cabbage family are troubled by root maggots.

Root maggots are more prevalent early in the spring, and by the time their season has passed, the newspaper will have disintegrated. An alternative treatment is to use diazinon.

Brussels sprouts are high in Vitamins A and B1.

CABBAGE

One of my favourite dishes is early cabbage, prepared in this simple way: core the heads, cut into wedges, gently steam or boil and serve with salt and pepper, butter or lemon juice. The secret to tasty cabbage dishes is to never overcook it. Green and savoy cabbages are excellent for this recipe, and for coleslaw. Red cabbages are favoured mainly for adding colour to salads. Late-maturing cabbages are grown specifically for long-term storage. They stay green for long periods in storage, mature very late in the season, and have thick, coarse leaves. Storage cabbage is too heavily cored to be used for sauerkraut or cabbage rolls. Many of the hybrid varieties are superior to traditional varieties of cabbage: they result in a better yield, have a high resistance to pests and are less affected by weather conditions.

RECOMMENDED VARIETIES

Emerald Acre • small cores, very tender; superb flavour;green; matures early.
Prime Choice • short cores, very tender; fine-textured leaves; matures mid-season.
Stonehead • best mid- to late-season variety for sauerkraut, cabbage rolls; blue-green
Meteor • red cabbage; compact heads with small veins; matures mid- to late-season.
Canada Savoy • elegant, ruffled leaves, deep greens heads; stores well; matures
mid- to late-season.
Houston Evergreen • good storage cabbages; heavy green heads; matures late-season.

Meteor   Prime Choice

BEFORE YOU PLANT

• Cabbages are heavy feeders, and do best in rich, well-drained soil. Work compost or well-rotted manure into the soil. If you are seeding, sprinkle bonemeal along the rows before adding seeds; if you are transplanting, add one handful per plant.

• Try to choose a site where cabbage, broccoli, Brussels spouts, cauliflower, kale or kohlrabi were not planted for at least two years. This helps to eliminate problems with soil-borne diseases.

Experiment with these herbs when using cabbage in the kitchen: basil, caraway, cayenne pepper, cumin, dill, fennel, marjoram, sage, savory.

WHEN TO PLANT

• Cabbage can be seeded outside from April until June. Light frosts will not harm the young plants.

• For the earliest crop, start seeds indoors the first week of April and transplant outdoors at the beginning of May. If you are buying plants from a greenhouse, it is important to choose small plants. Seedlings which have been growing in a conatiner for more than six weeks will not produce full-sized heads.

HOW MUCH TO PLANT

• Expect a yield of 3/4 to 3 pounds (1.5 - 5.5 kg) per plant.

PLANTING METHODS

• Sow at fingertip depth.

• Plant seeds 1 to 2 inches (2.5 - 5 cm) apart in rows or squares.

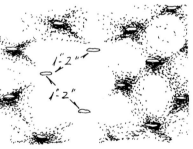

GROWING TIPS

• Let plants grow to a good size before thinning, as you are likely to lose some to insects. Thin to 8 inches (15 - 20 cm) between plants, to allow room for proper head formation. The young plants that are removed can be used as spring greens — a delicacy in salads.

• Cabbage has shallow roots. Do not cultivate deeply near the plants, and try to keep cabbages well-watered during periods of drought.

• A sudden burst of growth can cause cabbages to split, although this is not a severe problem with mid- to late-season varieties. Splitting is prevalent in certain varieties when heavy rain follows a long dry spell. I remember years ago, on rainy days in the summer, the sound of heads splitting in the field, often so loud the cracks could be heard from the yard outside the house.

HARVESTING

- Harvest cabbage at whatever stage you like: loose-leafed for sauerkraut and cabbage rolls, or leave it grow until heads are tight and solid.
- Once in a while, if the season is long and favourable, early cabbages will form a secondary crop of quite small heads after the central head has been cut, in much the same manner in which broccoli grows. To allow this to happen, just leave the plant to grow after making your harvest.
- At your final harvest, pull up the entire plant, roots and all. Cut off the roots, chop them and add to your compost bin.

STORAGE

- For storing, early cabbages are poor, mid-season varieties are better and late cabbages are best.
- Store cabbages inside a mesh bag in a cold room or cool garage; humid conditions and temperatures near freezing are ideal.
- Keep early cabbages, unwashed, in the crisper drawer of a refrigerator; use within two weeks. When using for cooking, trim conservatively as outer leaves are extra rich in nutrients.

Early cabbage has a small core, tender, succulent leaves and is best to use for cabbage rolls and sauerkraut.

PROBLEMS

How can I control cutworms?

Cutworms generally surface in the late evening. The easiest and most effective method for control is to till the soil around the plants. This brings the cutworms to the surface where they can be destroyed. Warm, dry conditions in the late summer provide favourable egg-laying conditions for the adult moths, resulting in increased numbers of larvae the following year.

Keep plants well-watered and the soil moist throughout the season to deter cutworms.

What should I do about root maggots?

To prevent root maggot problems, cover the soil with newspaper, as close to the plants as possible. This prevents the parent flies from laying eggs in the soil at the base of the plants; if they leave their eggs on the newspaper, the eggs will dry out in the sun and die. If you do not like the looks of newspaper in the garden, you can buy root maggot "collars" from a garden centre which are more aesthetically pleasing.

Cabbage is rich in vitamins B1 and C, and a good source of minerals.

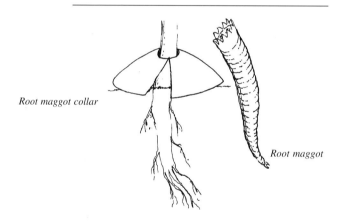

Root maggot collar

Root maggot

Cabbage, Beef and Tomatoes

A quick and tasty dish for times when you are in a hurry.

1 3/4 lbs. (700 g) lean ground beef
3 or 4 medium onions, chopped
1 medium cabbage, chopped
1 one-quart (1 L) jar or large tin canned tomatoes
1/3 cup (80 ml) ketchup
Salt and pepper to taste

Brown ground beef, drain. Add onions and cabbage and cook gently until translucent. Stir in tomatoes and ketchup, sprinkle with salt and pepper and cover. For variety, add basil or oregano. Simmer 20 to 30 minutes. Serve with baked potatoes. Makes seven servings.

CARROTS

Carrots are one of the most versatile vegetables. You can plant them from early spring to early summer, and again in late fall. They can be grown in a small or large garden, in a patio planter or window box. In your kitchen, feature them in every course of the meal, from juice to salad to dessert.

RECOMMENDED VARIETIES

Nantes 616 • my all-time favourite carrot; sweet, coreless and juicy; never needs peeling; matures early. For the home gardener, a Nantes-type carrot is the best choice. Nantes are medium-sized, blunt-ended carrots, the very best for eating fresh and juicing, but a type rarely found in supermarkets because they break easily.

Baby Sweet • very sweet and juicy; coreless; no peeling required; matures early. Babay types can be considered a novelty. They are sweet, juicy and mature early, like Nantes, but with such short roots, the amount of food reaped per square foot is less.

Imperators • the traditional carrot; can be woody and dry, so I do not grow them.

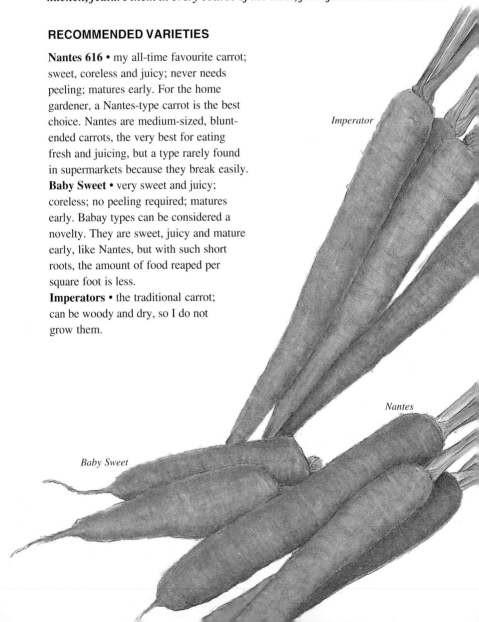

Imperator

Nantes

Baby Sweet

BEFORE YOU PLANT

• Work the soil just deeper than the length of a mature carrot; soft soil allows roots to develop uniformly.

• Get rid of weeds; carrots are relative weaklings and will lose the battle against tough weeds.

• Never add fresh manure; it may produce rough, hairy roots and will cause forks and splits. If fresh manure has been added to the soil, wait until the next growing season to plant any root crop; well-rotted manure is fine.

• Try this trick: mix radish seed with your carrot seed before sowing. Vigourous radish sprouts will easily push up through the earth, breaking the way for the carrots. Radishes mature earlier, and as they are harvested, space is left for the carrots to grow. Emerging radish seedlings will also mark the rows for you.

WHEN TO PLANT

• Sow early; carrots can withstand several degrees of frost.

• Seed at least twice; I prefer three times: once in late April, in the third week of May and around the 10th of June. Sow no later than mid-June if you want a full-sized crop. I have seeded as late as June 25th for a nice late crop of baby carrots.

HOW MUCH TO PLANT

• Generally, one packet of seed sows 30 feet (9 m) of row.

• Seed quite thickly; germination is usually only about 80 per cent. Thickly-seeded carrots will help one another push through the ground.

PLANTING METHODS

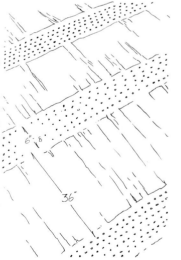

• Sow at fingertip depth.

• Plant three close rows, spaced 2 inches (5 cm) apart.

• This ideal pattern is difficult to obtain by hand; you can dribble the seeds off the end of a trowel, or just scatter it in a band 6 to 8 inches (15 - 20 cm) across. In a large garden, a precision seeder is easy to use and will give a similar result.

Meadow Seeding

• Scatter your seed in a 1-foot-wide (30 cm) band to create a miniature meadow of carrots. This method works well in a small garden.

Plant in Fall

• Experiment with a fall seeding, in late October. Prepare the ground well before seeding, and sow twice as thickly and twice as deep as usual, since germination will be less than if seeded in spring. You will have carrots ready for eating two to four weeks earlier than a spring-planted crop.

GROWING TIPS

- Carrot seed needs to stay damp for many days before sprouting. Sprouts will not push through dry, crusted soil. Cover the rows with finely sifted compost to insure good germination, especially in late season plantings.

- Try this simple method to reduce future weeding. A week after planting, take a rake, point the prongs at the sky, and very lightly stir the soil where you have just seeded. Germinating weed seeds will be exposed to the air and die; freshly-sown seeds have not yet germinated and will be fine.

- After planting, walk an empty wheelbarrow along the rows to lightly firm but not overpack the soil over the seeds.

- Never thin carrots, except when you want to eat them. Tiny carrots are an exquisite treat when lightly cooked and served with butter, salt and pepper. You can also use them in soup, salads and stews. Thinning carrots is just extra work and really does not need to be done.

- Adequate watering is most important from the time seeds are sown until the root swelling begins, a couple of weeks after seedlings emerge. Water during periods of drought; a downpour on dry soil may cause carrots to split.

Experiment with these herbs when using carrots in the kitchen: anise, basil, chervil, chives, cinnamon, cloves, cumin, dill, ginger, marjoram, mint, parsley, sage, savory, tarragon, thyme.

HARVESTING

- Bright orange roots will tip you off that harvest may begin; the deeper the colour, the more beta-carotene is present.

- One crop of carrots can be harvested for months, long past the "maturity" date marked on the seed packet. Pull early for tender "baby" carrots, and leave others in the ground until you are ready to use them.

- Carrots still in the ground will not be harmed by frost. Tops may die off and exposed crowns may be damaged, but the majority of the root will be fine. Complete the harvest before the ground freezes and sticks to the roots.

Misshapen carrots.

STORAGE

- Cut green tops off half an inch (1 cm) above the crowns. Wash immediately after pulling. Split or damaged carrots should be used in the kitchen within a few days or discarded; store only the sound, healthy ones in a humid, cold area, with temperatures just above freezing.

- To store in the refrigerator, place clean carrots between paper towels inside perforated plastic bags. Carrots can also be stored outdoors: fill a plastic pail with carrots, dig a hole in the garden, and cover with layers of newspaper. Carrots will keep in this manner until Christmas.

- Inspect stored carrots often, and immediately throw out any carrots showing signs of decay, to reduce spread.

Carrots contain a large amount of Vitamin A.

PROBLEMS

What causes green or purple crowns?

This is a sign of exposure to sunlight during the growing season. You can prevent this discolouration by covering the exposed crowns with soil, and sowing more thickly. Carrots are still fine for eating and storage, although frost-damaged carrots may turn mushy — check your store occasionally and throw out any carrots showing signs of rot. My favourite variety, Nantes 616, stays deep in the ground, minimizing this problem.

Why are my carrots misshapen?

An inconsistent supply of water is the likely cause. Carrots also become forked and twisted in attempting to push through heavy clay or compacted soil.

Wash carrots as soon as possible after pulling. They are easiest to clean fresh from the ground.

CAULIFLOWER

Cauliflower is often considered the most delicious of the cabbage family. It is a cool weather crop, sometimes difficult to grow because it is easily affected by hot, dry weather and is attractive to pests, but still a very worthwhile vegetable to include in your garden. The self-wrapping types are less work, but they mature later. Purple-headed types have a slightly different flavour, turn green when cooked, and are treated more like broccoli in the kitchen. The leaves of purple- and green-headed varieties do not have to be tied over their curds while growing.

RECOMMENDED VARIETIES

Extra-Early Snowball • an early crop; be prepared to cover the curds as soon as they open, harvest promptly.
White Rock • matures about two weeks later; nice, solid white curds; self-wrapping.
Burgundy Queen • adds intriguing colour to salads and raw vegetable plates.
Alverda • a bright lime green curd both raw and cooked.

Extra-Early Snowball

White Rock

BEFORE YOU PLANT

- Cauliflower needs a rich, well-drained soil. Add a generous amount of compost or well-rotted manure to the planting area.
- Try to choose a site where no members of the cabbage family were planted for at least two years.

WHEN TO PLANT

- If you are starting plants indoors, seed in the first week of April and transplant outdoors at the beginning of May. If you are buying plants from a greenhouse, choose small plants. Seedlings which have been growing in a container for more than six weeks will not produce a good crop.

Experiment with these herbs when using cauliflower in the kitchen: basil, caraway, chives, cumin, dill, garlic, marjoram, parsley, rosemary, savory, tarragon.

HOW MUCH TO PLANT

- Most plants yield about 1 to 2 pounds (500 g - 1 kg).
- I recommend planting a minimum of six each of an early, mid-season and late variety, for a continuous supply.

PLANTING METHODS

- Transplant just slightly deeper than plants were growing in their containers.
- Set the plants 6 inches (15 cm) apart in rows or squares. Closely-spaced plants tend to hold their leaves straight up, which helps to protect the growing curds.
- To prevent root maggot problems, cover the soil with newspaper, as close to the plants as possible. This prevents the adult flies from laying eggs in the soil at the base of the plants.

Cauliflower is high in vitamin C .

GROWING TIPS

- Keep plants well-watered and fertilized throughout the season to ensure proper development of curds. Failure to do so may result in heads being spotty and discoloured, leafy, "ricy", very tiny or not developing at all.

- To keep cauliflower heads white and tasty, the leaves must protect the curds from sunlight. On plants which are not self-blanching, you can tie the leaves to enclose the heads. At this point, it is only a matter of days until they are ready for harvest — **you must check them daily**. The warmer the weather, the faster the plants mature.

- Use different-coloured strings to help you keep track of maturing crops: for example, red ties for the early variety, blue for the mid-season, and so on. In this way you will know at a glance which ones should be harvested first.

Always keep a close watch on enclosed heads!

- In larger gardens, it is easier to simply break the leaves over the top of the curds. The result is not as pretty, but it does save time and effort. I usually use this method in my garden for even a small crop.

The leaves of the Extra-Early Snowball must be tied up to keep the curds snowy-white.

HARVESTING

- When ready for use, the heads are compact, very firm and snowy-white, even across the top. It is better to harvest cauliflower when heads are small and solid, about three-quarters of their mature size. Heat and maturity causes heads to loosen, discolour and develop a strong flavour.

To save time, cook broccoli and cauliflower together, but leave the pan uncovered.

STORAGE

- Do not remove outer leaves. Cut a thin slice from the stalk, and store cauliflower in the crisper drawer of the refrigerator. Cauliflower keeps for ten to 14 days.
- Cauliflower can be made into sweet pickles mixed with cucumbers and onions, or on its own. Some people like dilled cauliflower; use the dill pickle recipe for cucumbers and simply substitute cauliflower florets.

PROBLEMS

Why did my cauliflower produce only tiny heads at maturity?

Your seedlings were probably too old when planted out. Seedlings which are transplanted when older than six weeks tend to form only a tiny head, or "button". Unstable weather conditions such as cold temperatures at transplanting or dry spells can also cause this condition. In very hot weather, heads may not form at all.

I did not cover my cauliflower in time, and the heads turned yellow.

Slightly yellowed curds can be pickled, or you can try adding a bit of milk to the cooking water to whiten them. Discoloured cauliflower can be used but often has a strong flavour.

Basic Cauliflower ─────────────────────────────────

Plain and simple is best for savouring the flavour of fresh vegetables.

Place cauliflower in a saucepan with a small amount of water and bring to a boil. A bit of milk may be added to whiten curds. Cook covered for only a few minutes. Take care not to overcook. Drain, sprinkle with salt and freshly ground black pepper; add butter or lemon juice. Occasionally I top it with a white cream or cheese sauce.

CELERIAC

Both celeriac and celery are grown in the same manner, and have a similar taste, although celeriac has a more nutty, zesty flavour. The former is slightly less work to grow, as it needs a lot of water but not to the extreme demanded by celery. Celeriac has a large, round, knobby, turnip-like root with white, almost fibreless flesh. Use it to enhance soups, or to add flavour to vegetable juices, stews and salads. Celeriac is also known as celery root, celeri-rave, and turnip-rooted celery.

RECOMMENDED VARIETIES

Large Smooth Prague • a good variety; tasty roots are fairly free of lateral stems.

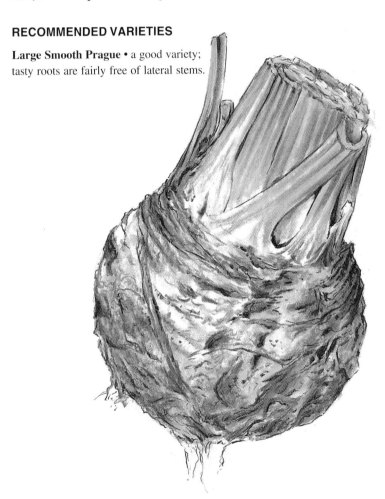

BEFORE YOU PLANT

• Choose a site which is easy to water. Unless you keep this crop well-watered throughout the season, both yield and quality will be compromised.

• If you are buying plants from a garden centre, be sure that you are selecting celeriac rather than celery. Both plants look the same when young. If you are growing both crops, you might plant them in the same location for ease of watering. Celery requires consistent, heavy watering, but celeriac plants will not be harmed if watered to the same extent.

WHEN TO PLANT

• Transplant outdoors from the middle to the end of May, once seedlings have two true leaves. Celeriac will tolerate light frosts.

HOW MUCH TO PLANT

• Put in at least one dozen plants.

Experiment with these herbs when using celeriac in the kitchen: basil, oregano, parsley, tarragon.

PLANTING METHODS

• Celeriac needs a long growing season. If you plan to seed, you must start the plants indoors. Just press seed onto moist soil surface, and keep well-watered.

• Transplant celeriac into a shallow trench 2 to 3 inches (5 - 7.5 cm) deep, with 6 inches (15 cm) between plants.

Celeriac is very low in calories and contains vitamin B, iron and calcium.

GROWING TIPS

• This crop must be kept well-watered and fertilized throughout the season. Never allow soil to become dry.

• Remove side-shoots and withered lower leaves.

HARVESTING

- Harvest celeriac in the late fall. Generally I dig this crop shortly after the final potato harvest. The longer you leave celeriac to grow, the bigger the roots will become.

STORAGE

- Keep unwashed celeriac inside perforated plastic bags in the refrigerator to retain moisture. It will keep for a week or more. Large quantities should be stored like carrots and parsnips.

PROBLEMS

What are common problems with growing celeriac?

Celeriac is relatively trouble-free, provided it has a consistent supply of moisture and nutrients during the growing season. Keeping weeds under control also contributes to a better crop.

Celeriac

To serve celeriac on its own as a vegetable dish, cook it as you would a turnip. Celeriac is often difficult to peel; try slicing it first. The cut surface of raw celeriac darkens quickly when exposed to air. To retain its milky white colour, do not cut it until just before cooking, or cook the root whole, unpeeled, then peel and cut it after cooking. When you serve celeriac raw, rub the cut surface with lemon juice or vinegar.

Despite the difference in looks, celeriac and celery are in the same plant family. (Left to right: peeled celeriac root, celeriac plant and celery.)

CELERY

Celery is a demanding crop: it requires more water and nutrients than any other vegetable we grow, in an even supply throughout the season for optimum yield and quality. The best crop we ever had was after a rainy summer, during which we continued to water the celery. I have never tasted such sweet, wonderful stalks as those. There are really only slight differences in varieties of celery, other than days to maturity.

RECOMMENDED VARIETIES

Utah 52-70 Improved • a nice, uniform, dark green variety that matures early.

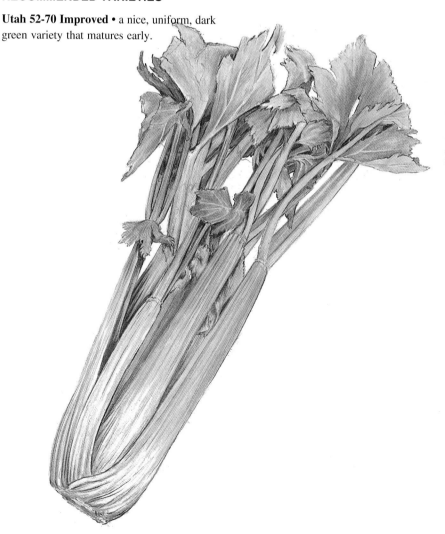

BEFORE YOU PLANT

• Choose a site which is easy to water. Unless you keep this crop well-watered throughout the season, both yield and quality will be compromised.

WHEN TO PLANT

• Transplant outdoors from the middle to end of May, once seedlings have two true leaves. Celery will tolerate light frosts.

HOW MUCH TO PLANT

• Put in at least one dozen plants to provide enough fresh celery for a small family throughout the summer.

PLANTING METHODS

• Celery needs a long growing season. If you plan to grow celery from seed, you must start the plants indoors. Fill seedling containers with a potting mix, press the seed onto a moist soil surface, and keep well-watered.

• Transplant celery into a shallow trench 2 to 3 inches (5 - 7.5 cm) deep, with 6 inches (15 cm) between plants.

Experiment with these herbs when using celery in the kitchen: basil, curry, dill, nutmeg, parsley, tarragon.

GROWING TIPS

• Celery needs a lot of water, uniformly supplied throughout the season. If growth is slowed for any reason, the stalks turn tough, stringy and bitter. Always keep soil moist; be prepared to water every single day.

• It used to be common practice to hill up soil over growing stalks, to "blanch" celery during the growing season, for the purposes of creating paler, more tender hearts and stalks. I have always considered this a messy and unnecessary chore, and am glad to see it falling from favour. To me, celery is just as tender, and much more nutritious and flavourful left to grow naturally.

HARVESTING

• During the growing season, break just one or two stalks from the outer edge of plants as you need them.

• While plants are growing, you can trim away green leaves, and use them for adding flavour to soups. Cut no more than one-quarter of the growth.

• To harvest, cut the entire plant just above the base of the root.

STORAGE

• Cut a thin slice from the base. Store celery inside a plastic bag in the refrigerator; use within two weeks.

Celery contains vitamins A and B, and is a good source of minerals. Garden-fresh celery is usually better than store-bought for using in salads, soups and on raw vegetable platters. Celery can be served on its own, braised and glazed in the oven, or boiled and flavoured with herbs and served au gratin or with a cream sauce.

PROBLEMS

Why were my celery plants small?

Celery needs much more water and nutrients than almost any other vegetable. Prolonged dryness at the roots has obvious and devastating effects, causing not only small plants, but also inedible hearts.

Celery trimmed to the way stores like it, with the top growth chopped and side shoots removed.

CORN

Hybrid corn varieties can be separated into three categories: standard, sugar-enhanced and super sweet. Standard sweet corn varieties (SU) have the traditional corn flavour, and quickly begin to convert sugar to starch once cobs are picked. Sugar-Enhanced (SE) varieties have been modified to increase sweetness and retain tenderness. Super Sweet hybrids (SS) have been further modified to produce the highest sugar content of all the corn types, and to retain their sweetness the longest in storage.

Seed is more expensive for the Sugar-Enhanced and Super Sweet types; both require extra care to produce quality cobs. Cobs of Super Sweet varieties are also slightly smaller and the kernels are slightly tougher; some people find them too sweet as well. Which type is the best-tasting is a matter of personal preference.

RECOMMENDED VARIETIES

Buttervee • SU; "traditional" corn flavour; one of the best-tasting standard varieties; matures very early.

Extra Early Super Sweet • SS; superb flavour; matures mid-season.

Maple Sweet • SE; sweet, tender kernels; matures early.

Precocious • SE; a choice variety; matures very early.

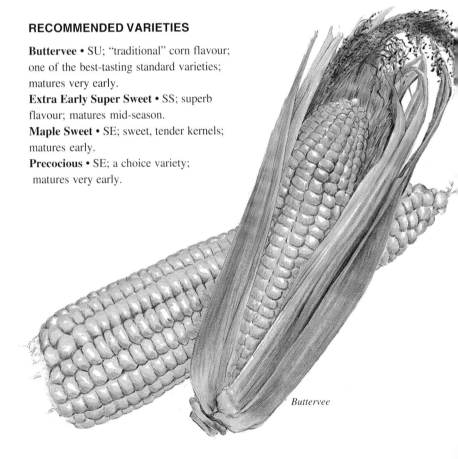

Buttervee

BEFORE YOU PLANT

- To successfully grow Super Sweet varieties, you must follow these rules:
  - Isolate from other types to prevent cross-pollination, otherwise very starchy, tough kernels will result. Separate by spacing 25 feet (7.5 m) apart, or by timing, so that between varieties, there is a minimum ten day spread between expected maturity dates. Do this by planting varieties with different maturity dates at the same time, or by planting varieties with the same maturity dates at different times.
  - Use fungicide-treated seed or delay planting until soil is warm; avoid planting in soils below 55°F (13°C) or the seed could rot.
  - Do not plant in dry soil; Super Sweet seed needs twice the moisture to germinate as normal corn.
  - Make a smooth seed bed; planting at a uniform depth is critical with Super Sweet seed.
- All types of corn need a highly fertile soil with good drainage. Work a generous amount of compost or well-rotted manure into the soil before sowing.
- Corn is tall and can shade other crops. Plant it on the north or east side of your garden, or next to shade-tolerant crops such as leaf lettuce and spinach.
- Try to choose a location where corn was not planted the year before, especially if you had a severe insect or disease problem with previous crops. An ideal site is where beans or peas were planted last season; corn will benefit from the nitrogen-enriched soil provided by these leguminous crops.

Corn is a good source of vitamins A and B3.

WHEN TO PLANT

- Plant corn from early to mid-May. If using untreated seed for early plantings, sow twice as thickly (likely only half the seed will make it). Do not sow untreated Super Sweet seed until the soil is warm.

HOW MUCH TO PLANT

- Expect to harvest from 30 to 36 cobs from a 10-foot (3 m) row.
- If you have room, plant more than one variety. In a small garden, plant at minimum eight seeds.
- The sweeter the corn, the more attractive the seed is to insects that live in the soil; compensate by sowing more thickly.

Experiment with these herbs when using corn in the kitchen: chervil, chives, lemon balm, saffron, thyme.

PLANTING METHODS

- Sow seeds to the depth of your second knuckle. Super Sweet seed should be planted less deeply than other types; sow only to the depth of your first knuckle.

- Sow seeds 2 inches (5 cm) apart; allow for thinning. Corn must be planted in double rows to permit cross-pollination; space rows 2 feet (60 cm) apart. Alternative patterns for small gardens are blocks or hills of eight seeds. Plant different varieties in different areas. Isolate Super Sweet varieties.

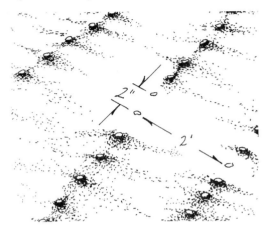

- If you have room to grow only a small amount of corn, consider buying started plants from a greenhouse. Transplanting seedlings into the garden gives you a jump on the season, and eliminates the problem of seed decay.

When cooking corn-on-the-cob, always prepare more than you will need for that meal. Simply strip the kernels off the leftover cobs, place them in a plastic bag and store in the freezer.

GROWING TIPS

- The easiest way to thin corn is to use a hoe. Simply flip out the unwanted seedlings; leave a "hoe width" between plants. Transplant thinnings to fill in gaps caused by seeds which did not germinate.

- Keeping the corn patch free of weeds is important. After plants are a foot tall, cultivate shallowly to avoid damaging roots, and hill the soil around the stalks.

- Be prepared to cover young seedlings with jute sacking if there is a risk of frost. This measure has given us a crop in many years when other people had none.

- Adequate watering is most important during ear formation — from the time tassels appear until the ears are ready for harvest.

HARVESTING

- The length of time it takes for corn to ripen varies greatly according to planting dates and weather conditions. When corn matures depends primarily on temperature. The optimum temperature for corn is 90°F (32°C). The closer the average daily temperature is to that ideal temperature, the sooner the corn will mature. The "number of days to maturity" noted on seed packets is most accurately used to compare varieties.

- Harvest when kernels are full and "milky", generally indicated by drying and browning of ear silks. Corn is ready to eat from 18 to 24 days after silks first show; the warmer the weather, the sooner you can pick it.

- Try to pick corn just before you are ready to eat it. Corn is at its most sweet and tender when eaten the same day as it is picked.

- Attempt to cover corn plants if there is a risk of frost. Severe frost will kill a corn plant. Super Sweet cobs will last on the plant weeks past a frost. Standard sweet corn will lose flavour within three to four days of a frost, if not picked. Sugar Enhanced varieties last somewhere in between — about one week.

STORAGE

- Cool temperatures slow down the conversion of corn's natural sugars to starch, and help keep corn sweet and juicy. If possible, plunge corn into ice water immediately after harvest, and then refrigerate. Leave husks on the cobs; if they have been removed, store the cobs inside a plastic bag. For ultimate quality, eat corn the day it was harvested.

PROBLEMS

What causes corn plants to topple over and ears to fall off?

*Check the stalks for holes and small worms; the likely cause is the **corn borer**. These insects are difficult to control without using chemicals. Regular spraying of rotenone or pyrethrum (a botanical insecticide derived from chrysanthemum flowers) may help. Destroy any borers that you see. Onions and chives are reputed to have a repellant effect. Remove affected corn stalks in the fall, because these insects can survive over winter on the plants.*

Why are there missing kernels on my cobs?

The cause is likely improper pollination, which can occur if corn is planted in single rows, or if a very heavy rainfall occurs at the time of pollination. Some varieties do not develop full kernels at the tips of cobs.

Poke a thumbnail into a kernel to test for juicy, ripe corn.

CUCUMBERS

Long English, European or greenhouse cucumbers grow best in a greenhouse and are favoured for their length and thin, edible skins. Pickling types taste great eaten fresh, and often do not need to be peeled. Pot cucumbers are so-named because they spread to only half the size of most cucumbers and grow well in patio pots. Slicing cucumbers are smoother, darker and longer than pickling types, and must be peeled unless they are very young and tender.

RECOMMENDED VARIETIES

Long English
Corona • tasty, dark green cucumbers; can grow 10 to 12 feet (3 - 3.5 m) tall; requires pruning and staking.

Pickling
Spear-it • abundant yields; uniform size; dark green, warty fruit; white spined.
Pioneer • heavy yields; uniform; dark-green fruit; black spined.

Pot
Bush Pickle • the best bush-type cucumber for containers; plants half the size of most vining types; tasty fruit 4 to 5 inches (10 - 12.5 cm) long.

Slicing
Sweet Slice • amazingly sweet, crisp, juicy flesh; one of the longest and smoothest-skinned outdoor cucumbers; a "burp-less" variety, popular with people who normally cannot eat cucumbers.
Supersett • smooth tapered fruit; excellent disease resistance; tremendous yields.
Dasher • long slim cucumbers; heavy yields; compact plants.

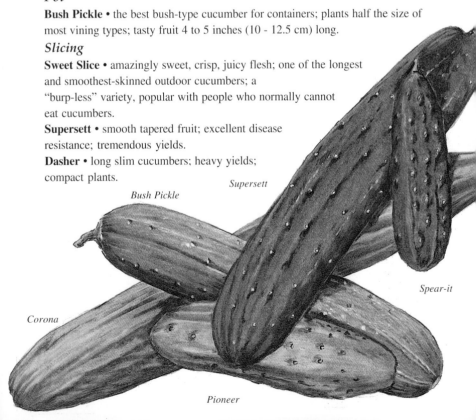

Supersett

Bush Pickle

Spear-it

Corona

Pioneer

BEFORE YOU PLANT

• Cucumbers yield a lot of fruit, therefore they require extra fertilizer. Work in a generous amount of compost or well-rotted manure, and add a fertilizer high in nitrogen and potassium.

• If you choose a sunny spot next to a fence, the cucumbers will use the fence as a support for climbing, and benefit from the shelter the fence provides.

• Cucumbers can also be planted fairly close to corn. The corn protects the cucumbers from wind, and traps heat, which cucumbers love.

WHEN TO PLANT

• Seed cucumbers into warm soil at the end of May or first week of June. You can protect young seedlings with hot caps against cold; crops sown early must have this protection. Temperatures anywhere close to freezing will kill unprotected seedlings.

• Transplant seedlings outdoors from the end of May until the end of June. Use hot caps to protect plants and help them grow more quickly. If you cut a slit at the top, the plant will grow through the hole and the hot cap can be left on. Otherwise, remove it when foliage touches the top. Water well and fertilize before covering with hot caps.

HOW MUCH TO PLANT

• Expect to harvest about ten cucumbers per plant from most varieties. Many of the hybrids yield twice as much.

• Greenhouse cucumbers usually produce about 25 fruit per plant.

PLANTING METHODS

• Sow seed to a depth slightly less than your first knuckle.

• Cucumbers are easiest to look after when planted in hills. Sow five to seven seeds per hill, and allow 12 to 18 inches (30 - 45 cm) between hills. If you are planting in rows, allow 4 to 5 inches (10 - 12.5 cm) between plants, and 2 feet (60 cm) between rows.

Pickling varieties are best for making dill pickles, but other types can also be pickled. Slicing varieties are usually used for bread-and-butter, nine-day and sweet pickles.

TRANSPLANTING

- If you have started your cucumbers indoors or bought plants from a greenhouse, follow two important rules for transplanting outside:

    1. Wait for warm weather before transplanting (late May to early June).
    2. Take care not to disturb the roots when transplanting.

- Lift the plants carefully from the containers and very gently set them into planting holes at the same depth they were growing

in their original containers. I find it better to cut the casing away if plants are in a cell-pack, rather than to tip it upside down. Lightly firm the soil around the plants, and water immediately. Feed with 10-52-10 "starter" fertilizer once a week for the first three weeks after planting.

CUCUMBERS IN CONTAINERS

- Most people put only the pot varieties into containers, although any type of cucumber can be grown in this manner. Support plants with stakes or a trellis, and water and fertilize them regularly. Cucumbers can be grown in a hanging basket very successfully, although you must be extremely diligent with watering and fertilizing for good results. The containers should never be allowed to dry out.

GROWING TIPS

- Water around the base of the plants, not over them, and try to do so early in the day to allow plants to dry before nightfall. Avoid splashing dirt onto the leaves; many diseases are harboured in the soil and can be transferred to foliage in this manner.

- Watering is most important just after seeding and during fruit production. Drought can cause low yields, bitterness and hollow fruit.

- Cucumbers are one of the few vegetables that I thin. Leave this task as late as possible in the season, about mid-June, as you are bound to lose some plants to cold weather or cutworms. Cucumbers are extremely sensitive to cool temperatures.

- The first fruits from pickling varieties are absolutely the best. Make these into wonderful dill pickles.

- When the plants first begin producing fruit, it is important to pick off each fruit when it reaches about 3 inches (7.5 cm) in length. Removing that first fruit can nearly double the subsequent yield.

- Stay away from the cucumber patch first thing in the morning and whenever the plants are wet. Their vines are brittle early in the day, and easily damaged; handling wet or damp cucumber plants can spread diseases. Wait to weed until later in the day and plants are dry.

HARVESTING

• Harvest regularly to keep the vines producing. Cucumbers should be picked weekly to increase the yield.

To ensure pollination of hybrid cucumber varieties, seed companies generally add to each packet a few "monoecious" seeds, that produce plants with both male and female flowers. These seeds are marked with a harmless coloured dye.

• To avoid disease, never pick cucumbers first thing in the morning or after a rainfall. The best time for harvest is late morning or early afternoon.

• Cut fruit from the stem with a sharp knife,and support the plant with your other hand. Pulling at vines or tugging on fruit can damage the plants. Never flip them; this can cause injury or death.

STORAGE

• Do not wash before storing. Wrap cucumbers in plastic cling wrap or tightly in plastic bags, and keep in the refrigerator; use within a week.

Cucumbers are a good source of iron and vitamins.

• If you decide to store your cucumbers for a day or two until you have enough for pickles, do not refrigerate them. Quality deteriorates quickly in the refrigerator; a cool basement or root cellar with a temperature about 50 - 60°F (10 - 15°C) is best for short term storage.

Ripe Cucumber Pickles

A wonderful use for big, over-ripened, yellow & orange cucumbers!

10 - 12 large ripe cucumbers

Peel and cut cucumbers down centre; scrape out all seeds and soft pulp. Cut into wedges and let stand in a light brine of 1/2 cup (125 mL) coarse salt and enough water to cover. Leave for 6 hours. Drain and rinse

Boil for 10 minutes:

> 4 cups (1 L) vinegar
> 2 cups (500 mL) water
> 2 cups (500 mL) sugar
> 4 Tbsps. (100 mL) pickling spice

Put cucumber wedges into the boiling mixture for about 15 minutes; lift out when transparent. Place wedges into a jar; add one chili pepper per jar if you like hot pickles. Repeat procedure until all wedges are cooked. Fill jars to top with remaining hot liquid and seal.

PROBLEMS

What causes cucumbers to become bitter?

Any disruption in their growth can cause bitterness — cool weather, lack of moisture or lack of fertilizer. Try to keep the plants well-watered during periods of drought. Bitter cucumbers are safe to eat; however, you may not care for their taste.

Why do my cucumber plants have spots on their leaves?

Cucumbers are susceptible to several diseases that cause spotting on both foliage and fruit. Rain splashing on the soil transfers diseases from the soil to the plants; try mulching with peat moss before the vines spread to provide a "splash barrier", and always water around the base of the plants, not over them. Stay away from the cucumber patch whenever the plants are wet.

Pickles

Young pickling cucumbers are best for crunchy pickles, but they lose moisture and become soft within a day or two of being harvested. To avoid compromising the quality of pickles, prepare your brine in advance. As soon as you have enough cucumbers to fill a jar, heat the brine and pour it hot over the pickles. Seal, store, and wait a few days until more cucumbers are ready for harvest. For best results, try to pickle within 12 hours of harvest. Wash the fruit just before pickling.

For dill pickle brine, use 1 cup (250 mL) sugar, 2 cups (500 mL) coarse salt, 6 quarts (5.5 L) vinegar, and 10 quarts (9.5 L) water. Boil for five minutes and pour hot into jars filled with cucumbers, dill weed and garlic (one to two cloves per jar). Seal well and store.

To add colour, insert whole yellow beans or small carrots into the spaces between cucumbers before adding brine; these pickles look pretty and make a wonderful gift.

Cucumber vines can be allowed to spread along the ground, or trained up a stake or trellis.

EGGPLANT

Eggplant, or aubergine, is a tropical plant that has ornamental as well as food value. It needs a long, hot summer in order to grow well, so it may perform marginally in northern gardens. The "standard" eggplant bears glossy black fruit; however, there are interesting varieties with pink, green, white or yellow fruit in a variety of shapes.

RECOMMENDED VARIETIES

Blacknite • the best of the larger-fruited, oval types; plants hold the deep purple fruit off the ground; high yields.
Dusky • smaller, pear-shaped, black-purple fruit; high yields; matures earlier than Blacknite.

Blacknite

Dusky

BEFORE YOU PLANT

• Eggplant does best in a warm, sunny, sheltered spot. Choose a site which receives about eight hours of sun each day. A south-facing location near a wall is perfect.

• If you are planting in containers, top them up with fresh potting soil each year for the best results.

WHEN TO PLANT

• Transplant into the garden in early June, when the weather is warm.

Eggplant is a good source of Vitamin B2.

HOW MUCH TO PLANT

• For the first attempt at growing eggplant, start with two to three plants. If you are a great fan of this vegetable, put in six plants. Expect to harvest about four to five pounds (1.8 - 2.2 kg) per plant.

PLANTING METHODS

• Prepare a hole for each plant. Pinch off some of the lower leaves and place plants into the holes, slightly deeper than they were growing in their original containers.

• Allow 8 to 12 inches (20 - 30 cm) between plants.

• Eggplants are pretty plants with attractive lilac flowers and wonderful glossy fruit. Consider planting them in your flower bed, or in a large patio container. Three plants grow nicely in a 12-inch (30 cm) container; remember to water and fertilize potted plants more often than those in the garden. A few French marigolds potted with the eggplant add colour and may repel insects.

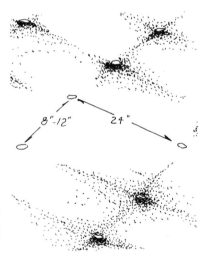

GROWING TIPS

• Eggplants can be staked like a tomato plant, to support the plant against wind and help hold long fruits off the ground. When staking, try to set the support on the prevailing downwind side of the plant, so that the plant will be protected against the support in strong winds.

• Put in the stakes immediately after transplanting. Drive them about 1 foot (30 cm) deep in the soil, approximately 3 to 5 inches (8 - 12.5 cm) away from the plant.

HARVESTING

- Harvest whenever the fruit is a satisfactory size and the skin is still glossy. Twist the fruit from the plant like picking an apple, or snip fruits off with shears. Pick regularly to encourage further production.
- Dull skin is an indication that the eggplant is overripe, and becoming tough and bitter.

Experiment with these herbs when using eggplant in the kitchen: basil, cinnamon, dill, garlic, marjoram, mint, oregano, parsley, sage, savory, thyme.

STORAGE

- Keep eggplant uncovered, in the refrigerator; use within five days.

PROBLEMS

How can I control Colorado potato beetles?

These beetles are bright orange-red with black stripes, and can completely defoliate a plant within a few days. If the infestation is slight, simply hand-pick or knock them into a container; be sure to remove the beetles, larvae and eggs. Otherwise, spray with rotenone at the first sign of damage. Garlic and marigolds are said to have a repellant effect.

Eggplant is a basic ingredient in ratatouille, a French vegetable dish, and moussaka, a Greek lamb stew. Stuffed eggplant makes an impressive display , served between stuffed red and green peppers. Experiment with eggplant in place of pasta in your favourite lasagna recipe.

To prevent eggplant from discolouring, sprinkle or rub cut surfaces with lemon juice.

GARLIC

Garlic is a wonderful crop for the home gardener, fairly easy to grow and relatively trouble-free. It takes up little space and can be tucked in amongst your flowers, as long as it is given a sunny spot.

Most people plant regular garlic, although you can grow the elephant type. Its cloves are sweeter, milder and larger than regular garlic (up to half a pound (250 g) each).

Elephant garlic is fussier to grow and takes up more room in the garden. It can be eaten as a vegetable on its own, steamed with a cream sauce, but unlike regular garlic, the elephant type must be kept at temperatures below freezing to slow shoot development, and it will only store for a short while.

Garlic chives are a wonderful variation on standard chives — they have the same mild onion flavour with a light touch of garlic. Experiment with these as a substitute for garlic and chop them into salads along with the dainty star-like flowers for a pretty display. Garlic chives are also known as Chinese chives — by either name, this is a good compromise for those who like garlic's flavour but not its pungency.

BEFORE YOU PLANT

- Separate bulbs into cloves and plant only the large, firm, healthy ones.

- If you are planting in the summer, you can set the garlic in the garden amongst growing vegetables. The sunnier your site, the larger the bulbs are likely to grow.

- Try to choose a spot where garlic or other plants in the onion family were not recently grown. Garlic also needs a well-drained soil; water sitting at root level can cause rotting or disease.

- Sprinkle bonemeal in the planting area to help strong roots develop.

WHEN TO PLANT

- The secret to growing large bulbs is the planting date: the best time to plant garlic is in late August for a harvest of large bulbs the following year.

- You can also plant in spring, the earlier the better. If the frost is out of the ground in the first week of February, put the cloves in the ground. They will not be harmed if the weather turns cold again — garlic can freeze and still grow when the weather warms.

HOW MUCH TO PLANT

- Each clove grows into a new bulb containing 10 to 20 cloves.

- The largest cloves produce the largest bulbs. Save the small cloves at inside of bulbs for use in the kitchen.

Garlic contains Vitamin B1 and minerals.

PLANTING METHODS

- Push each clove into the ground to the depth of your second knuckle, firm the soil around it and water. The pointed end must be up, or it will not grow.

- Allow 2 to 3 inches (5 - 7.5 cm) between cloves in rows, squares, raised beds or containers.

Why buy garlic sets?

- Garlic sets are bulbs carefully selected for planting. They are ready to sprout, will grow more quickly and produce larger bulbs than garlic sold for culinary use. While the garlic sold on grocery shelves can be planted, these bulbs have been chosen specifically for culinary use, and can take longer to sprout and grow.

Be sure to leave the pointed end of clove facing up.

GROWING TIPS

- Feed with a high nitrogen fertilizer in spring when leaves begin to grow. Pull out any weeds to reduce competition for moisture and nutrients.

- When flower stalks appear in early summer, snip off the flowers to allow the plant to devote more energy to the developing bulbs. Save the flowers for a pretty and zesty addition to salads and vegetable dishes.

- Stop watering shortly before harvest. Allowing the soil to dry out around the maturing bulbs will improve storage quality.

Garlic & Roses

- Garlic is reputed to be a good companion to other plants for its insect-repelling qualities. I find that the garlic actually does better when planted near roses, probably because it has a nice sunny location, and benefits from the constant watering and fertilizing that the roses receive.

- A lady I know plants garlic throughout her vegetable garden, and tucks a few plants in her flowerbeds. She uses no insecticides and has very few problems with bugs. I am sure the reason is the interplantings of garlic.

HARVESTING

- Allow tops to fall over on their own. Bending down tops in the late summer can delay rather than promote early maturity, by causing new shoots to form.

- Garlic is ready for harvest when the leaves are withered and dry, usually in September. Harvest bulbs as soon as they mature; left too long in the ground, they begin to separate and will not store properly.

- Pull or dig plants out and leave them on top of the ground for several days, weather permitting. If the weather is not warm and dry, allow plants to dry in a warm, dry basement or garage.

STORAGE

- Allow garlic to dry before storing. Roots may be rubbed off when they are dry and brittle, although this is not necessary. Either braid the garlic, tie it in bunches or cut off stems 2 to 3 inches (5 - 7.5 cm) above the bulbs. Do not wash or separate cloves.

- Store on slatted shelves or screens. In the kitchen, keep a small supply of bulbs in a wire basket, garlic pot or any other container which allows air circulation. Do not store in the refrigerator.

- To braid garlic for storage, allow the tops to dry on the plant. Braid the tops just as you would your hair; add whatever you like for a decorative touch, or leave it plain.

PROBLEMS

Why were my bulbs so small when harvested?

You probably planted too late in the season. Garlic needs a long growing season — five to six months — in order to mature to a good size. Add a handful of bonemeal when planting to encourage growth.

Why does my stored garlic begin to sprout indoors?

Probably the storage conditions are too humid. Garlic should not be kept in the refrigerator. The bulbs may have been too moist prior to storage — garlic must be extremely dry in order to store well.

The garlic inside the jar of my home-made pickles has turned blue.

Sometimes the cloves will react to the brine and turn blue or purple. Certain varieties always undergo this colour change. Do not be concerned — this is entirely natural.

Here are some tips for using garlic in the kitchen:

- To make a clove easier to peel, squash it with the flat side of a knife.
- If you need a large quantity of garlic for a sauce, simmer the cloves in water or bouillon for a few minutes. Remove from water; the skins will easily slip off.
- To remove the smell of garlic from your hands or a cutting board, rub the surface with half a lemon.
- As a general rule, the longer garlic cooks, the sweeter and more mellow its flavour becomes. Be careful not to let it burn or it will become bitter.

Sweet Garlic Salad Dressing

This recipe is especially good for the early season's first salad greens.

1 whole garlic bulb
1 Tbsp. (25 ml) white wine vinegar
1 Tbsp. (25 ml) extra-virgin olive oil
1 Tbsp. (25 ml) safflower oil
Dab of honey
Freshly cracked black pepper

Separate and peel garlic cloves; place in saucepan with enough water to cover, bring to boil, reduce heat and simmer until tender, about 15 minutes. Remove garlic cloves, increase heat and boil liquid until only 2 Tbsps (30 ml) remains. Put cloves in sieve, pour hot liquid over them, mash through into a small bowl using back of wooden spoon. Whisk vinegar and oil into garlic, flavour with honey and pepper.

Garlic braided for storage.

KALE

Kale (borecole) is a wonderful vegetable for beginning gardeners, as it is not fussy about soil conditions and is rarely troubled by pests, unlike other members of the cabbage family. This vegetable is very tolerant of frosts, can be harvested even in the snow, and withstands summer heat. Kale is very popular in Holland. To the uninitiated, its flavour may be an acquired taste. It is among the most nutritious of vegetables; use it in the kitchen as you would spinach — cooked, or raw in salads. Kale is marvellous for adding colour and flavour to a hearty soup of beans, squash and leeks.

If you grow ornamental kale in the garden, cut plants at the base and set in a vase of water for a long-lasting "cut flower." Many restaurants use the vegetable kale for ornamental effect, as a garnish for salad bars or on the plate in place of parsley.

RECOMMENDED VARIETIES

Green Curled Scotch • an elite strain; bushy plant; yellowish-green curled leaves; great taste.

BEFORE YOU PLANT

• Unlike other members of the cabbage family, kale will tolerate poor soil conditions and heavy frosts.

WHEN TO PLANT

• Kale can be sown in early April. The seedlings are very tolerant of frosts.
• If you are very fond of this vegetable, seed a second crop for a late fall harvest.

HOW MUCH TO PLANT

• Expect a yield of about 2 pounds (1 kg) per plant.

Experiment with these herbs when using kale in the kitchen: bay, curry, dill, garlic, marjoram, hot peppers.

PLANTING METHODS

• Sow at fingertip depth.
· Plant seeds 1 to 2 inches (2.5 - 5 cm) apart in rows or squares.

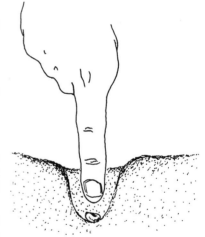

GROWING TIPS

• Kale grows like leaf lettuce, there is no need for thinning.

HARVESTING

• Begin to harvest kale when the leaves are 6 to 8 inches (15 - 20 cm) high. Cut a few leaves at a time, as you would with leaf lettuce.

• Kale is least bitter when the leaves are young and tender; its flavour is often enhanced after a couple of good frosts.

STORAGE

• Store unwashed inside a plastic bag in the refrigerator. Use it within two weeks.

Kale is one of the best sources of vitamins A, C, iron and folic acid.

PROBLEMS

What are common problems with growing kale?

Kale is less troubled by pests than other members of the cabbage family, although it can be plagued by flea beetles or root maggots. For methods of treatment, see **Beets** and **Brussels sprouts**.

Cooked Kale

Kale's robust flavour compliments foods such as sausages and bacon.

Remove any tough leaves and chop before cooking. Place kale in a saucepan with a small amount of water and bring to a boil. Cook covered for only a few minutes. Take care not to overcook. Drain, sprinkle with salt, freshly ground black pepper, lemon juice or a flavoured vinegar. For variety, top with a white cream sauce.

Ornamental or flowering kale and cabbage are most often grown as decorative plants. These handsome plants are not recommended for eating as their flavour is quite bitter.

KOHLRABI

Kohlrabi is one of four vegetables that I recommend for children to grow, along with carrots, peas and tomatoes. Kohlrabi is relatively trouble-free, easy to grow, and looks like something from outer space. When cooked, kohlrabi combines the best qualities of turnip and cabbage; raw, its flavour and texture are similar to that of a water chestnut. Kohlrabi can be peeled and eaten like an apple, or cut into sticks and served with carrots and a dip. This vegetable is fairly uncommon in our area of the world, but very popular in various regions of Germany. There are purple and white varieties of kohlrabi. Purple varieties mature slightly later. I like to interplant both types for a colourful display.

RECOMMENDED VARIETIES

Grand Duke • small plants; evenly-shaped bulbs; good weather tolerance; matures early.
Early White Vienna • uniform plant; short tops and few leaves; round bulbs.
Early Purple Vienna • Leaves and stems are purple-green; flat, globe-shaped bulbs with reddish-purple skin and white flesh.

*Early
Purple Vienna*

*Early
White Vienna*

BEFORE YOU PLANT

• Work compost or well-rotted manure into the soil.

WHEN TO PLANT

• Kohlrabi can be seeded outside from April until June. Light frosts will not harm seedlings.

• For the earliest crop, start seeds indoors the first week of April and transplant outdoors at the beginning of May.

• Grow only a small amount the first year. If you discover that you really like kohlrabi, plant three successive crops, with three to four weeks between seedings.

HOW MUCH TO PLANT

• A 10-foot (3 m) row will yield from 30 to 60 globes.

PLANTING METHODS

• Sow at fingertip depth.

• Thin to 4 inches (10 cm) between plants. Closely-spaced plants will have an increased yield of small, tender globes.

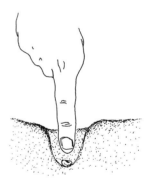

GROWING TIPS

• Maintain even moisture levels to prevent globes from splitting.

HARVESTING

• Harvest kohlrabi between the size of a golf ball and a tennis ball. The best globes are tender enough to be easily pierced by a fingernail. Larger globes can be used after removing the tough and fibrous portions.

• The central leaves are tender and taste delicious raw or cooked along with the globe.

STORAGE

• Keep kohlrabi inside a plastic bag in the refrigerator; use within two weeks.

Try using kohlrabi in any stir-fried recipe, and on a raw vegetable platter, served with a dip. I have introduced many people to kohlrabi in this manner — more often than not, kohlrabi is the favourite vegetable on the platter.

PROBLEMS

What causes kohlrabi globes to split?

Fluctuation in moisture levels can cause splitting, which is more prevalent in widely-spaced plants. Water during periods of drought, and plant so that the kohlrabi is slightly crowded in the row.

Vegetable Medley

Experiment with different vegetables for subtle changes in flavour.

Chop kohlrabi, parsnips, carrots and rutabaga. Place vegetables in a saucepan with a small amount of water and bring to a boil. Cover and cook for only a few minutes. Drain, add butter, salt and freshly ground black pepper. This dish can be served with a white cream or cheese sauce.

Use a butcher knife or hatchet to remove kohlrabi's tough stems.

LEEKS

The high price of leeks at the grocery store makes it worthwhile to consider planting this vegetable in your garden. The leek is really a large, upright, non-bulbing type of onion, which is milder, more hardy, and easier to grow. It withstands cold temperatures, is generally untroubled by pests and will grow in a less fertile soil. Leeks need a long growing season and require some work during the growing season. When cooked, this vegetable lends a creamy texture to soups and broths. To eat raw, chop leeks and add cherry tomatoes for an elegant salad, topped with an oil-and-vinegar dressing, and flavoured with fresh tarragon.

VARIETIES

Titan • the only variety which will result in a good stand from a seeded crop in northern gardens. All other varieties need a longer growing season and must be transplanted into the garden.
Unique • extra-long, thick shafts; matures early; stores well.

Titan

WHEN TO PLANT

• Leeks should be planted as early as you can get into the garden. Seedlings are not harmed by light frosts. The earlier they are planted and the longer they have to grow, the bigger the shanks will be.

• If you are seeding Titan into the garden, do so as soon as the ground can be worked, which is usually sometime in April.

• Large transplants result in the best leeks.

HOW MUCH TO PLANT

• Put in at least two dozen plants. Greenhouses often sell this amount or more in one container, and the resulting crop will be enough leeks to provide 12 to 15 meals for a small family.

PLANTING METHODS

• Sow seeds indoors, to the depth of the fingernail on your index finger, two seeds per inch (2.5 cm). Do this at the end of March, and transplant into the garden four to five weeks later.

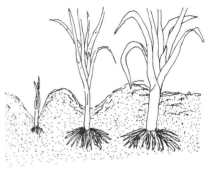

• Set plants into a trench as deep as your index finger, spaced 2 to 4 inches (5 - 10 cm) apart. As plants grow, gradually fill in the trench until it is level with the garden.

Gradually fill the trench as the plants grow.

Leeks must be dug up at harvest as their strong root system makes them difficult to pull. Dig up the entire plant, roots and all. Store upright in a cardboard box filled with soil, as if the leeks were growing.

GROWING TIPS

• During the growing season, hill the plants with soil two or three times, higher with each hoeing. This forces the growing point to the lowest leaves higher up the plant, the result being extra-long blanched stalks and a greater edible portion.

Leeks are a good source of vitamins.

HARVESTING

• In the late fall, dig up leeks, soil and all, leaving the roots intact.

STORAGE

• Place the entire plants upright with soil, into cardboard boxes, as if they were growing. Keep in a very cool location, such as a garage or coldroom, and pull out stalks as needed.

Experiment with these herbs when using leeks in the kitchen: cayenne pepper, chives, nutmeg, parsley, tarragon.

PROBLEMS

What are common problems with growing leeks?

Leeks are much less prone to problems than onions. Plant leeks in a rich soil and keep them well-watered and fertilized.

Leek & Potato Soup

2 oz. (55 g) butter
2 large onions, chopped
8 medium leeks, chopped
3 cups (750 mL) chicken stock,
   or water with 2 chicken bouillon cubes
2 medium potatoes, chopped
1 Tbsp. (50 mL) parsley, chopped
2 eggs or egg yolks
1/2 cup (125 mL) cream or milk
salt & freshly cracked black pepper

Melt butter. Sauté onions and leeks until golden. Add chicken stock, potatoes and parsley. Simmer for 30 minutes, mash or put through a seed mill, and return to pan. Blend eggs with the cream; add to soup and cook for a few minutes. Do not boil.

Season with salt and freshly cracked black pepper. Serve topped with parsley or chopped chives (in season). Makes four servings.

LETTUCE

Lettuce is easy to grow in a flower bed, patio container or salad patch in the vegetable garden. Plant a mixture of types to add pizazz to salads; most of these greens also come in shades of red. Butter (Butterhead, Boston, Bibb) lettuce has thick, tender leaves with a rich buttery taste, which are loosely shaped into heads. Head (Crisphead) lettuce has solid heads like cabbage. Leaf (Looseleaf) lettuce is my favourite kind of lettuce. It matures earlier than other types, and has much more vitamin A and C than head lettuce. Romaine (Cos) lettuce is the type most often used in caesar salads. Growing full heads of Romaine lettuce requires a fair amount of space; I find I get more greens for my salads by planting this type closely spaced, and harvesting it like leaf lettuce.

RECOMMENDED VARIETIES

Butter
Buttercrunch • crisper leaves than most butter varieties; remains sweet even after the plant has gone to seed; matures early.

Head
Gemini • deep green; excellent flavour; matures mid-season.
Ithaca • dark medium green; nice solid heads; matures mid-season.

Leaf
Brunia • reddish-brown; oak-leaf type; large, deeply-cut leaves; matures mid-season.
Fanfare • deep green; large, fringed leaves; matures early.
Red Sails • bronze red; large, ruffled leaves; matures very early.
Waldmann's Dark Green • dark green; large, fringed leaves; matures early.

Romaine
Parris Island 318 • larger and taller than most Romaine varieties.

Ithaca

Parris Island 318

BEFORE YOU PLANT

• Leaf lettuce is one of the few vegetables that can withstand partial shade. Crops in a slightly shaded area will grow somewhat more slowly, but will also be slower to bolt to seed in the heat of the summer.

• Lettuce will grow practically anywhere, but does best in a rich, well-drained soil.

WHEN TO PLANT

• Plant lettuce from very early spring to mid-July. I sow leaf lettuce at least three times, and use oak-leaf varieties for summer plantings, as this type is slower to bolt in hot weather.

• Sow head lettuce at least twice in spring, the first seeding as early as possible.

• All types of lettuce can be started from seed indoors; transplant seedlings into the garden when the leaves are about 1 to 2 inches (2.5 - 5 cm) long. The advantage with starting seeds indoors is that the lettuce will be ready for harvest very quickly, usually within three weeks of transplanting.

HOW MUCH TO PLANT

• Plant short rows to ensure that most of the lettuce will be consumed while the crop is at its peak.

Lettuce contains vitamins A and calcium. Romaine and leaf lettuces have a higher vitamin content than head and butter lettuces.

PLANTING METHODS

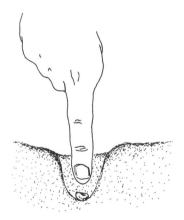

• Scatter seed along rows, and sow at fingertip depth.

• Plant in short, single rows or in a band up to one foot (30 cm) wide.

• Plant an early spring salad mix in your flower bed to add an edible as well as ornamental appeal to your garden. Mix different types of leaf lettuce — red, dark and light green — along with spinach, and in mid-May, sow in a sunny area. Leaf lettuce also grows well and looks lovely in a patio container.

• Experiment with a fall seeding of leaf or head lettuce, in the last week of October. Choose a sunny area in your flower bed, where you can plant bedding plants once the lettuce has been harvested. Prepare the ground well before seeding. Sow twice as thickly and twice as deep as you would in spring, as germination will be lower in fall-planted crops. You will have lettuce ready for eating from two to four weeks earlier than a spring-planted crop.

GROWING TIPS

• Thin head lettuce, and romaine if you want full heads to develop. Allow 8 to 10 inches (20 - 25 cm) between plants. Use the young plants you remove for tender salad greens.

• A steady supply of water is essential to produce crisp, tender leaves. Moisture is most critical for head lettuce when the heads are forming.

HARVESTING

• Twist off or cut leaf lettuce at ground level. Although leaf lettuce will regrow, it is better to sow successive crops. If, however, you have planted leaf lettuce in a container, cut it to about an inch (2.5 cm) above the soil, and allow it to produce a second crop.

• Harvest early in the morning when leaves are crisp and full of moisture.

• Pick only as much as you can use in two to three days.

STORAGE

• Pack leaf lettuce in layers between paper towels and place in a plastic bag, or simply wrap in a tea towel. Lettuce stays crisp for 2 to 3 days. Store all types of lettuce in the crisper drawer of your refrigerator.

• Rinse lettuce just before you use it. Very few outer leaves need be removed from garden lettuce, unlike lettuce purchased from a store.

PROBLEMS

What are common insect problems with growing lettuce?

Lettuce is one of the favourite targets for cutworms; see **Cabbage** *for methods of control. Aphids and slugs are other common insect problems; see* **Peppers** *to control aphids.*

How can I control slugs?

Place rinds of orange and grapefruit in the garden; the slugs will collect underneath and can easily be disposed of. Slugs will drown themselves in shallow containers of beer or honey. Diatomaceous earth (made from the pulverized remains of tiny fossilized ocean plants) sprinkled onto dry soil or foliage is an effective method of control; re-apply after a rainfall.

When I sliced my head lettuce, I discovered dry, black areas on the tips of the leaves. What could be the cause?

This is a condition called "tip burn", caused by water stress or calcium deficiency due to irregular or inadequate watering, especially when the heads are forming. Discard the black portions when preparing the lettuce. Regular watering and the addition of bonemeal to the soil around the base of the plants help to prevent this problem.

MELONS

Melons are interesting to grow, if you have plenty of room in the garden, and a hot, sunny location. If the season is warm and long, your reward will be mouth-watering melons, with incomparable vine-ripened flavour, and the satisfaction of successfully growing a fairly exotic, tropical crop in a northern garden. Always choose early-maturing varieties; the shorter the required growing season, the better your chances of success.

RECOMMENDED VARIETIES

Earlisweet • the best cantaloupe (musk-melon) variety for our climate; a high yield of melons with sweet, deep salmon flesh.
Earlidew • the best honeydew variety for northern areas; firm, slightly oval melons; very sweet, pale green flesh; fruit "slips" when ripe, like a cantaloupe.
Sweet Favourite • the best watermelon variety for short season areas; striped, oblong fruit; ripens early; very sweet, deep rose flesh.
Jack of Hearts • seedless watermelon; very sweet flesh; matures 2 weeks later than Sweet Favourite.

Earlidew

Earlisweet

BEFORE YOU PLANT

• Melons require a site which is hot, sunny, and sheltered from wind. Plant next to a fence, alongside corn, or provide a windbreak.

• All melons need well-drained, fertile soil. Slightly acidic soil is fine for watermelons.

WHEN TO PLANT

• Set transplants into the garden once all danger of frost has passed. Protect the young seedlings with hot caps; water well and fertilize before covering. If you cut a slit at the top, the plant will grow through the hole and the hot cap can be left on. Otherwise, remove it once the foliage touches its top.

HOW MUCH TO PLANT

• Plant a couple of each melon type, and be sure to select early-maturing varieties.

Melons are a good source of Vitamins B2 and C. Cantaloupes are higher in Vitamin A than other melons. Honeydew melons have the highest average sugar content of all melons.

PLANTING METHODS

• If you are starting seeds indoors, sow to the depth of your first knuckle. Allow at least four weeks before transplanting, until seedlings have their first set of true leaves.

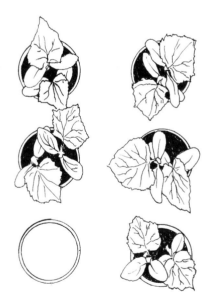

• Take care not to disturb the roots when transplanting. Lift the plants carefully from the containers and very gently set them into planting holes at the same depth they were growing in their original containers. I find it better to cut the casing away if plants are in a cell-pack, rather than to tip it upside down. Lightly firm the soil around the plants, and water well. Feed with 10-52-10 "starter" fertilizer once a week for the first three weeks after transplanting.

• Allow 8 to 12 inches (20 - 30 cm) between plants.

• Melons grow splendidly in large patio containers. Bush-type melons are the best choice, but vining types will do well if provided with stakes or a trellis to climb on. Water and fertilize regularly. The soil in the containers should never be allowed to dry out below the depth of your second knuckle.

GROWING TIPS

- Water around the base of the plants, not over them, and try to do so early in the day to allow plants to dry before nightfall. Avoid splashing dirt onto the leaves; many diseases are harboured in the soil and can be transferred to foliage in this manner.

- Moisture is most important in the early stages of growth and during pollination when fruits are setting. After this point, water only when the soil is very dry and leaves begin to show signs of wilting.

- Using hot caps early in the season encourages fruit to ripen sooner.

Melons do well under hotcaps.

- To increase your chances of getting sweet, ripe melons by the end of the season, do one of the following:
    - Pick off all new blossoms after three or four fruits have formed; or
    - Limit each melon runner to just one or two fruit, thus directing more of the plant's energy into fewer melons.

- Melons can be trained to grow on a trellis. Make tiny "hammocks" with pieces of cloth, nylon stockings or mesh bags, to carry the weight of the fruit and prevent them from breaking off or pulling the vines from their supports.

Seedless varities of watermelon require a longer growing season than other watermelons.

HARVESTING

• If possible, allow melons to fully ripen on the vine, for the ultimate in flavour, texture and sweetness. If there is a threat of freezing temperatures, however, pick off all good-sized fruit, or provide plants with protection from light frosts.

• With watermelons, look for these indications of ripeness:

  • As the melon ripens, the "ground spot" (where the watermelon rests on the ground) turns from white to a deep creamy yellow. The shiny surface of a watermelon dulls somewhat when it is ripe.
  • Knock on the melon with your hand. Immature watermelons make a sharp, ringing sound when rapped; ripe watermelons sound muffled.
  • Watch the watermelon stem to judge ripeness. When the tendril nearest the stem turns brown, dries up and curls like a pig's tail, the watermelon is ripe.

• With other types of melons, look for these signs:

  • A strong "musky" or "perfume" scent around the stem end of the melon indicates ripeness.
  • When the rind of muskmelons or cantaloupes changes from green to yellow or tan, and the netting pattern becomes pronounced, the melon is ready.
  • The stems on melons will separate or "slip" from the fruit with very little pressure as fruit ripens. A crack between the stem and fruit signals prime harvest-time. When the stem separates completely (a "full slip"), the melon is very ripe and should be picked and eaten soon afterward, before it becomes soft and mushy.

STORAGE

• Never store melons in the refrigerator. Cool temperatures cause them to lose flavour and texture, and they will not last as long or ripen as quickly as those kept at room temperature.

PROBLEMS

Why do my melon plants have spots on their leaves?

Melons, like cucumbers, are prone to several diseases which cause spotting on both foliage and fruit. Rain splashing on the soil can transfer diseases from the soil to the plants; try mulching with peat moss before the vines spread, and always water around the base of the plants, not over them. Stay away from melons whenever the plants are wet.

ONIONS

Onions may be planted in three ways: as seedlings, transplanted into the garden; seeded directly into the garden; or planted from onion sets. Starting seedlings indoors involves the most work; an alternative is to buy plants from a greenhouse, usually for less than the price of sets. Seeding is the least expensive method of planting, but also prone to the most problems. Onion sets are easy to plant, quick to mature and less plagued by pests, but are expensive. I recommend planting a combination of the three, to guarantee a good crop.

Scallions (bunching, salad, spring or green onions) are very hardy and take up little garden space. The roots are pulled before the bulb fully develops. They add colour and flavour to salads, sandwiches and relishes. Cooking onions have round, strongly-flavoured bulbs with tapered stems, and are excellent for cooking and storing. Red onions are especially valued, adding colour to salads and stir-fries. Spanish onions are ideal for salads, sandwiches, and French-fried onion rings. These onions are large, round and slightly flattened in shape. Spanish onions require such a long growing season that they must either be transplanted in spring, or seeded into the garden the previous year. Shallots produce small bulbs with a mild flavour. They are usually harvested earlier in the season than onions. Use shallots for cooking, garnishing or pickling. Pickling onions are mild, and need no thinning and little fertilizer. Onions from the mildest to strongest-flavoured, are: bunching, Spanish, red and cooking. In general, the drier the season, the stronger the flavour.

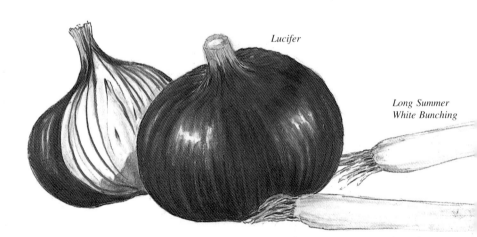

Lucifer

Long Summer
White Bunching

RECOMMENDED VARIETIES

Scallions
Long Summer White Bunching • long, white, mild-tasting shafts which mature very early.

Cooking Onions
South Port White Globe • the variety I most highly recommend; its large, white bulbs are the best for boiling and using around a roast, store extremely well and can be used as scallions when small.

Tarmagon • medium-sized, yellow bulbs with a strong flavour which mature very early and hold the most flavour when cooked.

Red Onions
Lucifer • blood-red bulbs; makes a good sandwich onion, and stores well.

Spanish Onions
Gringo • large, copper-coloured bulbs with small necks and sweet, white flesh.

Shallots
White Portugal • snow-white, tear-shaped bulbs.

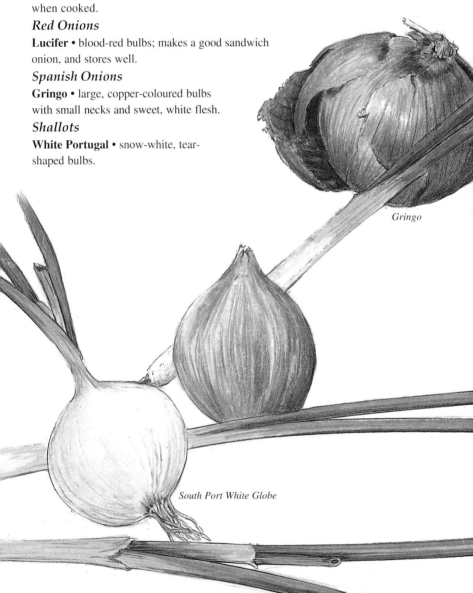

Gringo

South Port White Globe

BEFORE YOU PLANT

- Direct seeding requires a fine seedbed and good moisture conditions. Onion sets need good soil, but not the fine texture and high organic content demanded by a seed-sown crop.

- For transplanting, choose young, slender seedlings that are a healthy dark green. Onions transplant relatively easily.

WHEN TO PLANT

- Onions should be planted as early as you can get into the garden. Seedlings are not harmed by light frosts. The earlier they are planted and the longer they have to grow, the bigger the bulbs will be.

- The secret to growing great big Spanish onions is in the timing; plant your seeds or sets in late fall. Expect to lose some over a hard winter; plan to fill gaps with transplants in spring.

HOW MUCH TO PLANT

- In general, 1 lb. (500 g) of sets produces 30 to 40 lbs. (13.5 - 18 kg) of onions.

Young green onions are high in vitamin A.

PLANTING METHODS

Seed
- Sow seeds fairly thickly, to the depth of the fingernail of your index finger. To mark the rows, mix in a bit of radish seed. Radish seedlings will emerge more quickly than onions, and will mature and be eaten before onions need the space.

Transplants
- Lay the young plants in a trench and cover lightly with soil. The plants straighten themselves out.

Sets
- Press the sets into soft soil so that only the tip shows above ground. Plant scallions slightly deeper to get more white stem. To avoid trouble with root maggots, place the sets firmly on top of the soil, with only the root end underground. The most dependable sets are about 1/2 to 3/4 inch (1 - 2 cm) in diameter, about the size of marbles. Smaller sets take longer to grow.

To minimize problems place sets on top of the soil.

Onions and Flowers

- Green onions and milder-flavoured chives can be planted in flower beds, window boxes, pots and borders. Simply push in a few sets, sprinkle on some seeds, or poke in a few transplants amongst the flowers. These onions will grow very well, take up very little space, and your flowers may benefit from the onion's reputed pest-repelling qualities.

Fall Planting

- Experiment with a fall seeding, in late October. Sow twice as much seed as you would in spring-planting; germination will be lower in fall-planting. Prepare the ground well before seeding. You will have onions ready for eating in spring, from two to four weeks earlier than a spring-planted crop.

Experiment with these herbs when using onions in the kitchen: cinnamon, cloves, nutmeg, paprika, parsley, tarragon.

GROWING TIPS

- Onions which were seeded directly into the garden will require thinning. Wait until they reach a decent size. Use tiny thinnings like chives, and older ones as scallions in salads and to add flavour to cooked dishes.

- Cultivate often to control weeds; onions have shallow roots and do not compete well with weeds.

- Do not let onions dry out. This is especially important immediately after planting, and for the first six weeks of the growing season, to ensure proper bulb formation.

HARVESTING

- Harvest scallions any time during the growing season.

- Allow onion tops to fall over on their own. Bending down tops can delay rather than speed maturity: if the plants are not ready, they will put energy into developing new shoots rather than maturing bulbs.

- Pull onions and lay them on the soil right where they were growing. Leave them outside to dry in the sun for up to a week, until they are well-dried.

For fewer tears, peel onions under a stream of cold water.

STORAGE

- Separate onions into groups. Young and thick-necked bulbs should be used first, as they will not keep long. Onions are ready to store when skins rattle and necks are thin and dry.

- Store in a cool, dry area. Keep onions in a container which allows good air circulation, such as a shallow basket or mesh bag. Onions stored at room temperature will last from two to four weeks if kept dry. Green onions kept cool and moist in the refrigerator inside a plastic bag or standing in a glass of water will be at their best for only 3 to 4 days.

- To braid onions for storage, allow the tops to dry on the plant, and braid in the same manner as you would your hair.

PROBLEMS

I want to grow onions but I always have a problem with root maggots.

These pests can be avoided by planting onion sets. Place each onion set on top of the soil, and with a heavy hand, press it partway into the ground, until only the roots are buried. If you are using started plants, move the soil away from the growing bulb but keep the roots covered. This cannot be done with scallions.

As a general rule, when saskatoon bushes bloom, the adult flies are laying their eggs. Have controls in place. All members of the cabbage family are troubled by root maggots.

Sweet & Sour Onions

A tasty accompaniment to grilled steaks!

6 medium onions, thickly sliced	1 tsp. (5 ml) salt
1/4 cup (60 ml) cider vinegar	1/4 cup (60 ml) butter
1/4 cup (60 ml) sugar	1/4 cup (60 ml) boiling water

Lay onions in a shallow, greased casserole and sprinkle with salt. Combine vinegar, butter, sugar and water; pour over onions. Bake uncovered at 350°F (180 °C) for 30 minutes or until tender. Makes four servings.

For a milder flavour, substitute white vinegar for cider vinegar; for a sweeter dish, use a raspberry vinegar.

Onion tops will fall over on their own when these vegetables are ready for harvest.

PARSNIPS

Parsnips are one of the easiest root crops to grow: they are hardy, require little attention after planting, and can be left in the ground over the winter, for an early spring harvest of sweet, white roots.

RECOMMENDED VARIETIES

Harris Model • long, smooth, slim roots; uniform, tapered shape; on average, 12 inches (30 cm) long.

BEFORE YOU PLANT

- Parsnips need a deep, loose soil for roots to properly develop. Add compost or peat moss if your soil is hard, and work to the depth of 1 foot (30 cm), or deeper if you are growing a variety with longer roots.

- Never add fresh manure; it may produce rough, hairy roots and can cause forks and splits. If manure has been added to the soil, wait until the next growing season to plant any root crop.

WHEN TO PLANT

- Parsnips can be sown from as soon as you can work the ground up until early June.

Parsnips can be chopped or shredded for boiling, and simply flavoured with butter, salt and pepper. Whole parsnips can be scrubbed, the tops and ends removed, and cooked unpeeled with a roast in the oven.

HOW MUCH TO PLANT

- A 10-foot (3 m) row will yield about 15 pounds (7 kg) of parsnips.

PLANTING METHODS

- Sow seeds to the depth of the fingernail of your index finger.

- Plant in squares or three close rows, spaced 2 inches (5 cm) apart.

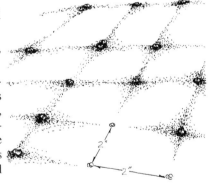

- Mix radish seed with parsnip seed before sowing. Vigourous radish sprouts will easily push up through the earth, breaking the way for the parsnips. Radishes mature earlier, and as they are harvested, space is left for the parsnips to grow. Emerging radish seedlings will also mark the rows for you.

- Experiment with a fall seeding, in late October. Sow twice as thickly and twice as deep as usual, to compensate for loss of viability over winter. Prepare the ground well before seeding. You will have parsnips ready for eating from two to four weeks earlier than a spring-planted crop.

GROWING TIPS

- Parsnip seed normally takes about three weeks to germinate. Do not allow the soil to dry out before the seedlings emerge.

HARVESTING

• Begin to harvest parsnips when the roots are the size of carrots.

• Harvest most of the crop in October. The flavour of the roots is improved after a couple of heavy frosts.

• Leave some roots in the ground over winter, and dig as soon as the soil thaws in spring. Overwintered roots will have a sweeter flavour.

STORAGE

• Keep in a cool place or in the refrigerator; use within four weeks.

Parsnips are high in vitamin A.

PROBLEMS

Why do my parsnips turn brown shortly after harvest?

The browning is likely an abrasion, a result of roots being roughly handled or scratched during harvest. This type of damage is most common in sandy soils. It is not a cause for concern; the roots are edible, although less attractive.

A garden fork is best for harvesting parsnips in hard soil.

PEAS

Fresh garden peas are irresistible — you simply cannot pick them without popping a few in your mouth along the way. In the years that we ran a pick-your-own operation, we always had a smile for the well-dressed women who would come down from the fields after picking peas with a ring of black soil around their mouths — evidence unknown to them of the alluring power of peas-in-the-pod.

There are basically two types of peas: shelling and edible-podded. Shelling peas are the traditional type of garden pea. Snow peas have flat, crisp, edible pods, which are harvested before they develop large peas, and are traditionally used in stir-fried dishes and salads. Sugar Snap peas are a unique class of edible pod peas, distinct from snow peas in that the pod walls are much thicker and that they are best for eating when the peas are regular shelling size. Sugar Snap peas may be eaten at any stage, and are less work to prepare for dinner than traditional varieties because no shelling is required.

RECOMMENDED VARIETIES

Shelling
Green Arrow • very sweet peas; long, bright green pods; high yields; easy to pick; mid-season.
Little Marvel • small, bright green pods; great flavour; early-maturing.
Patriot • very sweet; dark green pods; more peas per pod than Little Marvel; freezes very well; early-maturing.

Snow
Little Sweetie • bush type; small, tasty, bright green pods; stringless; early-maturing.

Sugar Snap
Sugar Ann • bush-type; sweet, crisp, medium green pods; wonderful flavour; high yields; mid-season.

Sugar Ann

Little Sweetie

Green Arrow

BEFORE YOU PLANT

• Inoculants are naturally-occurring materials that contain soil bacteria. They help pea plants extract nitrogen (a nutrient that is essential to growth) from the soil. Simply mix this dry, sooty powder with your seed before planting. Use a thick coating to increase yields. Buy inoculant fresh each year, and avoid exposing it to heat and sunlight. Excess inoculant can be worked into the soil.

• For early plantings, use *treated* seed, which is coated with a mild fungicide to prevent the seeds from rotting. If you are planting early into cool soil, and prefer not to use treated seed, sow more thickly, as some seed is likely to rot.

WHEN TO PLANT

• Plant as early as possible, as soon as you can get into the garden. Peas grow higher and develop more pods and more peas in each pod when days are long and relatively cool: the sooner planted, the better. Until they blossom, pea plants are not harmed by any but the heaviest frosts.

• Sow, at the same time, varieties with different maturity dates for a continuous supply of fresh peas throughout the summer. I like to plant three seedings, about two weeks apart, with the last summer crop sown no later than the third week in June.

• Keep in mind vacation dates and skip plantings that will mature while you are away.

HOW MUCH TO PLANT

• A 10-foot (3 m) row will yield about 10 pounds (4.5 kg) of peas.

• Planting both early and late-maturing varieties will extend your harvest.

PLANTING METHODS

• Sow seeds to the depth of your first knuckle.

• Seed peas thickly, one after the other, along a single row. Sow varieties with different maturity dates in side-by-side rows. Between the rows, allow about 18 inches (45 cm), or just enough room to walk.

Mixed Garden Peas

• If you have a small garden without the room to sow successive crops, try sowing several kinds of seed in one patch. A mixture of varieties which mature at different times will give you an extended harvest of tender, young peas.

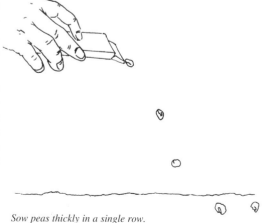

Sow peas thickly in a single row.

GROWING TIPS

- Peas are easiest to pick when the plants are staked, but they can be grown without supports. Letting the plants flop over on the ground is less attractive but also less work, and the yield is just as high — remember to be gentle with the plants when harvesting so as not to break the vines.

- Snow pea plants should be staked; otherwise, the pods are harder to pick.

- Seeds must remain moist after planting, and the plants need to be watered well from blossom time on, for optimum quantity and quality. Under dry conditions, peas are not as sweet.

Experiment with these herbs when using peas in the kitchen: chervil, chives, mint, rosemary, savory, tarragon, thyme.

Little Marvel has small pods which are ready for picking early in the season. Pick peas regularly to encourage further production.

HARVESTING

• Pick peas when they are young and tender for the best flavour. Peas which become too old for fresh eating should be left on the vine until dry, and used in soups.

• Snow peas should be picked while the pods are small and flat. Harvest regularly to increase the yield.

• Sugar Snap peas can be eaten at any stage, pods and all, without removing the string.

• Be gentle with the plants when picking peas. The vines are brittle and break easily, which causes the plants to stop growing, and the peas already on the vine to age quickly and become tough.

STORAGE

• Store peas in plastic bags in the refrigerator; preferably, use them the same day. If, however, this is not possible, freeze the raw, shelled peas inside plastic bags. This will preserve their wonderful, fresh flavour. Use the frozen peas within a couple of weeks.

Peas are rich in Vitamin A, and high in protien, relative to other vegetables.

PROBLEMS

What are the white, powdery patches on my pea plants?

Powdery mildew is the most likely culprit; this fungal disease is more prevalent in dry seasons. Sulphur dust can be an effective control. Remove severely diseased plants and bury them, to prevent the fungi from spreading further.

Rotate crops in the garden, plant resistant varieties, seed early in the season and keep plants well-watered during periods of drought.

My pea plants are stunted, losing their lower leaves and dying prematurely. What is wrong?

This sounds like root rot. Pull up and destroy severely affected plants to prevent spread of the disease. If the problem is severe, try not to plant peas or beans in that location for several years. There are no chemical controls available.

PEPPERS

Peppers (capsicum) are classified as either hot or sweet. Hot peppers include cayenne and celestial types; celestial are most often hotter than cayenne. Sweet peppers include bell and banana types; bell peppers have the familiar blocky shape while banana types look more like their namesake.

RECOMMENDED VARIETIES

Sweet

Better Belle • green bell; ripens to red; matures mid-season.

Butterfingers • yellow banana; ripens to red; excellent for pickling, freezing, fresh eating; early-maturing.

Sunbell • yellow bell; ripens to red; very sweet; compact growth; good for patio containers; matures mid-season.

Hot

Fire • celestial; one of the hottest peppers; green peppers ripen to red; matures mid-season.

Super Chili • celestial; hotter than cayenne; green chili peppers ripen to red; great for drying; high yields; mature plants are covered with small green chilies that turn red when ripe.

Super Cayenne • cayenne; matures to green early to mid-August; can ripen to red; very fiery hot taste; good fresh or dried; need more space than bell pepper varieties.

Jalapeño • cayenne; thick pungent walls; good fresh or pickled; green peppers ripen to red; a favourite for Mexican foods; ornamental; attractive in patio containers; matures mid-season.

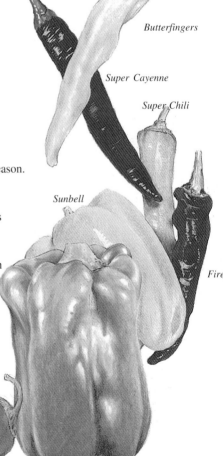

Butterfingers

Super Cayenne

Super Chili

Sunbell

Fire

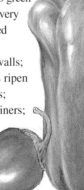

Jalapeño

Better Belle

BEFORE YOU PLANT

• Peppers do best in a warm, sunny, sheltered spot. Choose a site which receives about eight hours of sun each day. A south-facing location near a wall is perfect.

• If you are planting in smaller patio containers, use fresh potting soil each year for the best results.

WHEN TO PLANT

• Transplant into the garden in early June, when the weather is warm, and after all danger of frost has passed.

HOW MUCH TO PLANT

• Three to four plants is usually adequate. Expect a yield of 6 to 12 bell peppers per plant, 12 to 18 banana peppers per plant, and 30 to 40 hot peppers per plant.

Peppers are an excellent source of vitamin A and one of the best vegetable soures of Vitamin C.

PLANTING METHODS

• Pepper plants need a long growing season, so it is best to transplant seedlings into the garden. Sow seed indoors in early March, or buy plants from a greenhouse. Choose ones that are stocky and well-developed. Larger plants will produce fruit sooner than smaller ones.

• Prepare a hole for each plant. Pinch off some of the lower leaves and place plants into the holes, just slightly deeper than they were growing in their original containers.

• **Sweet:** Allow 8 to 12 inches (20 - 30 cm) between plants.

• **Hot:** Allow 15 to 18 inches (35 - 45 cm) between plants.

• Pepper plants are attractive and grow well in a flower bed or a large patio container. Three plants grow nicely in a 12-inch (30 cm) pot; remember to water and fertilize potted plants more often than those in the garden. A few French marigolds potted with the peppers add colour and may repel insects.

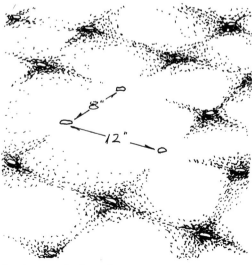

Sweet pepper planting pattern.

GROWING TIPS

• An even, adequate supply of water is most important during early fruit sizing. Inconsistent moisture (allowing the plant to dry out and then soaking it) or too little watering can result in smaller fruit and blossom-end rot. Water heavily at least twice a week, and every day without fail if the weather is hot and dry.

For a delicious seasoning, dry both sweet red bell and hot cayenne peppers, crush them and mix together. Use an empty spice jar as a shaker.

HARVESTING

• Pick the first peppers promptly as they reach full size to encourage further fruit set.

• Most varieties can be eaten green, or left on the vine to ripen to their mature colour.

• Pepper plants can be brought indoors at the end of the season. In a bright, sunny location, they may keep producing fruit until mid-December. Before bringing the plants indoors, first spray with an insecticidal soap to prevent bringing aphids into your home.

STORAGE

• Store peppers inside plastic bags in the refrigerator; use within a week.

• To dry hot peppers, simply string them with a needle and thread, and hang the "necklace" in a cool, well-ventilated area.

PROBLEMS

How can I control aphids?

These sap-sucking insects will not kill a plant, but they can weaken it severely. Spray with an insecticidal soap, and be sure to coat the undersides of leaves. Ladybugs devour aphids. Chives, garlic and nasturtiums are reputed to have repellent qualities.

Super Cayenne produces a high yield of fiery, hot peppers.

POTATOES

Even if you have a small garden, try to plant a few different kinds of potatoes: a very early, a russet, and a yellow-fleshed or a novelty type. If you have space, add a few mid- and late-season varieties.

The novelty types can be fun to experiment with. "Banana" or "fingerling" potatoes produce a heavy yield of highly-flavoured tubers with a unique shape. Some of the purple-skinned varieties also have purple flesh; surprise your dinner guests with exquisitely-flavoured, violet mashed potatoes. The yellow-fleshed varieties have a creamy, buttery texture and wonderful flavour.

RECOMMENDED VARIETIES

Warba • the earliest-maturing potato; round, white-skinned tubers; deep eyes; hard to clean; does not last long in storage.
Norland • the best variety for early harvest; matures slightly later than Warba; shallow eyes; excellent yield of tasty red-skinned tubers that store well.
Yukon Gold • mid-season; a favourite yellow-fleshed variety; large, oval tubers set near the top of the hill; stores well; excellent for baking, boiling and French Fries.
Kennebec • mid-season; fast-growing and high-yielding; white-fleshed, oblong tubers; stores well.
Russet Burbank (Netted Gem) • late-maturing; the best potato for baking and long storage; long, white tubers.

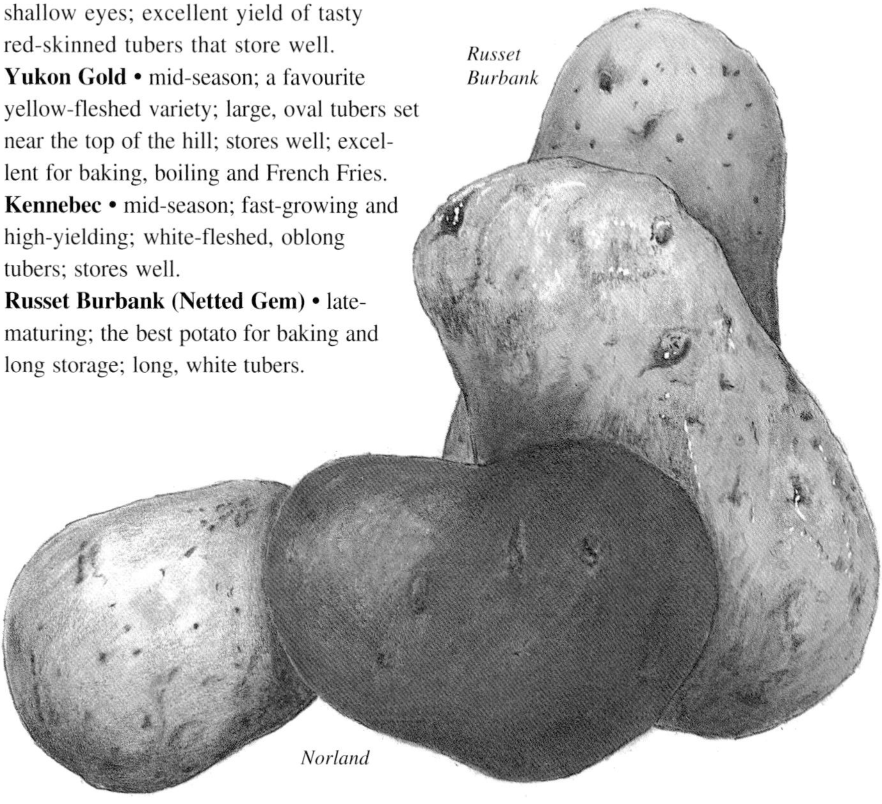

Russet Burbank

Norland

BEFORE YOU PLANT

- For faster emergence, keep seed potatoes in a warm (60° F/ 15° C) location for two weeks before planting. I use only whole tubers for the earliest plantings to reduce the incidence of rotting. Rotting often occurs when cut tubers are planted in cold soil.
- Potatoes are heavy feeders. Work composted or well-rotted manure into the planting area, or add a handful of bonemeal per plant. Do not use fresh manure or plant in an area to which lime has recently been added; these amendments encourage the disease called "potato scab".
- Try to choose a site where potatoes, tomatoes, eggplant or peppers were not planted for at least two years. If possible, plant potatoes in the area where your beans or peas were planted last year; they will benefit from the nitrogen-enriched soil provided by these leguminous crops.

WHEN TO PLANT

- Plant ten to 14 days before the average date of the last killing frost in spring. Potatoes can tolerate some frost, and it usually takes one to two weeks for the main stems and first leaves to emerge.
- If the weather is favourable, take a chance on producing an earlier crop by planting a small amount a week earlier.

HOW MUCH TO PLANT

- Five pounds (2.2 kg) of seed potatoes will plant a 50-foot (15 m) row, and yield about 2 1/2 pounds per foot (1.1 kg / 30 cm).
- If you plan to harvest your early crop all at once, you can re-plant in the same space with a later-maturing variety.

PLANTING METHODS

- Start with small, certified seed tubers weighing no more than 8 ounces (225 g). The ideal size for planting is about 2 to 3 ounces (55 - 85 g). Cut any tubers which are larger than that into equal pieces, ensuring that each cut piece has at least three eyes. Allow 24 hours for the cut to callous over; this reduces the chances of disease organisms invading the tuber.
- Plant each whole tuber or cut piece 4 to 6 inches (10 - 15 cm) deep. Set a seed piece every 8 to 12 inches (20 - 30 cm) along rows spaced 1 foot (30 cm) apart. Plan for one seed piece per hill. If you like small potatoes, space tubers 5 inches (12.5 cm) apart. For best results, cover planted seedstock with an inch or two (2.5 - 5 cm) of soil; do not tamp the soil.

Plant seed pieces 4 - 6 inches deep and ensure each has at least three eyes.

GROWING TIPS

- Hoe regularly during the growing season; frequent cultivation will aerate the soil and keep it weed-free.

- When plants are 6 to 8 inches (15 - 20 cm) tall, hoe up to 4 inches (10 cm) of soil between the rows to create hills. The soil temperature within the hills stays cooler than the soil surface, and is normally more ideal for tuber growth. Hills preserve moisture and keep tubers from being exposed to sunlight. Sunlight on exposed tubers can cause "greening", a condition that indicates a build-up of compounds which make the tubers inedible.

- Never hill potatoes when the plants are in bloom. Lateral shoots that produce tubers may be damaged, and the yield will be significantly reduced.

- Water regularly to ensure high yields, uniform growth, and better resistance to pest problems. During hot, sunny periods, water more often. A constant moisture supply is most important when tubers begin to form, about six to ten weeks after planting.

One medium cooked potato contains about 90 calories (377 kJ).
Potatoes are an excellent source of vitamins B1 and C,
dietary fibre and minerals.

HARVESTING

- Potatoes can be dug whenever they are large enough to eat. Blossoms are an indication rather than an assurance of maturity; some cultivars do not flower in some years. Small tubers can be dug during flowering or a few days afterward. Some people like to harvest a week or two after blossoms appear.

- To harvest a few potatoes without removing the whole plant, try this method: pull away some of the soil from the hill with your hand, and pull some tubers off at the roots. The plant will suffer little harm and continue to produce potatoes.

- Do not remove vines right after flowering. Vines and leaves produce food for storage in tubers, resulting in larger potatoes. Either wait for the vines to turn completely brown and shrivelled before harvesting, or cut them back in late August or September, once the potatoes have reached an acceptable size. Wait a couple of weeks after cutting the vines to dig the crop. At that point, the skins have *set* (they do not easily rub off), and the potatoes will keep for a longer period in storage.

- Leave harvested potatoes outdoors in a shaded area to dry, for an hour or so, prior to storing. Ensure that the tubers are not exposed to sunlight for more than a few hours, to prevent greening.

- Hills provide marginal protection against fall frosts; potatoes which are properly hilled are unlikely to be damaged. Tubers which have been frozen will deteriorate rapidly in storage. Discard them to prevent the spread of rot.

STORAGE

• *Curing* potatoes before storing them helps prevent dehydration and decay. After harvesting, store the potatoes in a dark, humid area, at about 60°F (15° C), with good air circulation through the pile or sacks.

• After ten days of curing, gradually cool the area to a final storage temperature of 40 - 50° F (5-10° C). If the storage room is cooled naturally, potatoes should be dug for storage only after the room is adequately cool. Never put cold potatoes into a warm store room because they may rot.

• Sort through the store once or twice over a two to three week period to remove decayed tubers. Properly stored potatoes will keep from four to nine months, depending on the variety. Those stored at room temperature are at their best for only about one week.

• Store new potatoes in the refrigerator; use within a week.

Experiment with these herbs when using potatoes in the kitchen: basil, caraway, chives, coriander, dill, fennel, lovage, marjoram, mint, oregano, parsley, rosemary, sage, tarragon, thyme. With new potatoes, dill, mint and parsley are wonderful.

This is an ideal mix of potatoes to grow in the garden. From left to right: Yukon Gold, Norland, Russet Burbank, Purple Purple and Banana.

PROBLEMS

My potatoes have crusty, scab-like lesions on their skin. What is wrong?

*This is likely **common scab**, a fungal disease that often occurs in alkaline soil. Scab generally does not affect the plant or tuber quality, but is unsightly. Reduce its occurrence by planting scab-free, certified seedstock, and resistant varieties where possible. Avoid liming soils.*

What causes potatoes to be hollow inside?

Hollow heart is the result of potatoes growing too quickly. This can be caused by too much nitrogen in the soil, or overwatering after a dry spell; the tubers are still fine for eating and storing. To reduce its occurrence, try switching to a 0-20-0 fertilizer, and avoid using fresh manure. Water regularly, evenly and thoroughly; space plants more closely together; and use small, whole seed tubers.

What causes potatoes to turn green and taste bitter?

Exposure to light is the only cause of green potatoes, either while growing, during harvest or in storage. Green tubers contain toxic alkaloids that must be removed prior to consumption. The simplest solution is to cut off any green portions from the skin or flesh of afflicted tubers.

Why do some potato vines get very tall yet have few tubers?

Potatoes respond to high levels of nitrogen by producing heavy vine growth and delayed tuber growth. Heavy applications of fresh manure may add an excessive amount of nitrogen to the soil. Excessive vine growth should not be cut off or trampled. Try using less fertilizer or one with little or no nitrogen, such as 0-20-0.

Why Buy Certified Seed Potatoes?
Certified seedstock is guaranteed to be free of the most serious diseases. Table potatoes from a grocery store may carry plant diseases and are usually treated with a sprout inhibitor which can delay or prevent sprout emergence.

What causes knobs and poorly shaped Russet Burbank potatoes?

This variety often forms large knobs on the tubers when moisture levels fluctuate. Irrigation or heavy rain following drought will promote renewed growth; however, instead of increasing overall size, the tubers will begin new growth in localized areas, and knobs develop. The best way to solve this problem is by maintaining uniform soil moisture during the entire growing season, especially during tuber growth, which starts well before the flowers appear.

What causes potato vines to turn yellow and die down early?

There are several conditions that cause this:

Maturity: *Early varieties may simply have reached maturity, similar to a wheat crop that turns yellow once it has matured.*

Early Blight: *Early blight is a foliar disease that starts as small, angular dark spots and results in rapid deterioration and complete browning of leaves and vines; treat with bordeaux mix (a mixture of copper, lime and water).*

What causes darkening after potatoes are boiled?

After-cooking discoloration is caused by a reaction between naturally-occurring chlorogenic acid and iron in the tubers. This condition is common in Norland potatoes, and the problem seems to be worse at higher latitudes.

To reduce this condition, cut potatoes for boiling in relatively small pieces and add a tablespoon (25 ml) of lemon juice to the cooking water.

What causes potatoes to fall apart when boiled?

*This condition is called **sloughing** (pronounced "sluffing") and is most common when "high dry matter" cultivars, such as Russet Burbank, are overcooked. Control by careful attention to the cooking pot and remove potatoes when they are done.*

What are the little dark spots on potatoes that will not wash off?

*This is a fungal disease common to potatoes, known as **black scurf**. It is seedborne and may also cause bronze colouring on leaves. The dark growth is not harmful; prevent by using new certified seed each year.*

Potato & Onion Soup

2 slices dry white bread	3 Tbsps (75 ml) soft butter
1 1/2 Tbsps (40 ml) grated Parmesan cheese	1 Tbsp. (25 ml) flour
1/4 cup (60 ml) finely chopped onion	2 cups (500 ml) milk
1/2 tsp. (3 ml) salt	1 Tbsp. (25 ml) chopped parsley
dash of nutmeg & white pepper	1 cup (250 ml) mashed potatoes

Remove crusts, and lightly toast bread on one side under broiler. Remove from heat, butter untoasted side and sprinkle generously with cheese. Return to broiler; heat until lightly browned. Cool, cut into 1/2 inch (1 cm) squares and set aside.

Melt remaining butter in a medium saucepan, add onion and stir until translucent. Stir in flour, salt, pepper and nutmeg. Add milk and bring to a boil, stirring constantly, until slightly thickened. Add potatoes; whip with wire whisk until smooth. Mix in parsley. Ladle into bowls, top with cheese croutons and serve. Makes two to three servings.

PUMPKINS

When most people think of pumpkins, jack o'lanterns and mouth-watering pies come to mind. Pumpkins can be enjoyed in many other ways as well: in hearty fall soups, delectable cheesecake, and muffins, and their seeds, baked until toasted, are a tasty, nutritious snack. The miniature varieties make attractive displays on the dinner table for special occasions, tasty additions to meals when baked and stuffed, and children love them. Any type of pumpkin growing in the garden is fascinating to children and adults alike; these plants grow at an amazing rate — under ideal conditions, they produce up to one foot (30 cm) of vine growth in a single day!

RECOMMENDED VARIETIES

Autumn Gold • an excellent variety for northern gardens; medium-sized pumpkins, about 10 pounds (4.5 kg) on average; brilliant orange.

Prizewinner • for those who like huge pumpkins; under ideal conditions, can reach 100 pounds (45 kg) in our climate; the best-looking jumbo pumpkin; dark reddish-orange.

Prizewinner

BEFORE YOU PLANT

- The soil should be rich and well-drained. A sunny spot which is sheltered from winds is best.
- These plants require a lot of space.

WHEN TO PLANT

- Transplant pumpkins into the garden in mid-May. Water well, and set hot caps over the young seedlings to protect them from cold temperatures.

HOW MUCH TO PLANT

- Expect to harvest from four to six pumpkins per plant.

To easily separate seeds from pulp, place the fibres into a bowl of warm water and leave for a few minutes. The seeds will float to the top.

PLANTING METHODS

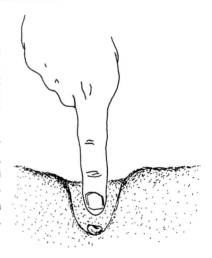

- Pumpkins take about 3 1/2 months from seeding to maturity. To ensure a nice-sized pumpkin for Halloween, it is best to transplant seedlings into the garden; you can, however, grow pumpkins by seeding directly into the garden.

- If you are starting plants indoors, sow seeds to the depth of your first knuckle, about three to four weeks before you plan to transplant them into the garden.

- Plant at least three seedlings or seeds in a hill; allow 6 feet (1.8 m) between hills.

Do not use a pumpkin for cooking after it has been used as a jack o'lantern: If you have used a burning candle inside the pumpkin, the carbon from the flame has built up on the inside of the pumpkin, making the flesh inedible. If you substitute a lit bulb for a candle, the warmth from the bulb and the exposure of the flesh to the air will encourage bacteria and mould.

GROWING TIPS

- When the plants are at least 2 inches (5 cm) high, remove all but the strongest two plants.
- Pumpkins must be watered and fertilized well throughout the growing season.
- To increase the chances of harvesting ripe pumpkins by the end of the season, do one of the following:
  - Pick off all new blossoms after three or four fruits have formed; or,
  - Limit each pumpkin runner to just one or two fruit, thus directing more of the plant's energy into fewer pumpkins.

Pumpkins are an excellent source of vitamin A .

HARVESTING

- Mature pumpkins are a deep, rich orange colour with skins that cannot easily be pierced by a fingernail.
- Cut stems with a sharp knife, taking enough stem for a good-sized *handle*.

STORAGE

- Only mature pumpkins with skin which cannot easily be pierced by a fingernail are suitable for storing. Keep them in a cool, dry, well-ventilated area. Do not store pumpkins on a cement floor or in an unheated garage.

The ideal time to harvest pumpkins is when they are almost completely orange.

PROBLEMS

Why are my pumpkins so small?

The cause could be seeding or transplanting too late in the season. Pumpkins need a lot of garden space, sunlight, heat and fertilizer for optimum development of fruit. A long, hot summer is ideal for producing the best crops. If you are intent on growing large pumpkins, limit each plant to only one or two fruit.

What causes rotten spots on pumpkins in the garden?

The "ground spot", where the pumpkin rests on the soil, may rot if it contacts a soil-borne disease. Try mulching with peat moss before the vines spread, and if the problem is prevalent, set empty coffee tins or some type of support under the growing fruit, to lift them off the soil.

Pumpkin   Cheesecake

This recipe puts ordinary cheesecake to shame!

1 pound (500 g) mashed pumpkin
2 1/2 lbs. (1.1 kg) cream cheese, softened
1 cup (250 ml) sugar
4 large eggs, lightly beaten
3 egg yolks, lightly beaten
3 Tbsps (75 ml) flour
2 tsps (10 ml) ground cinnamon
1 tsp. (5 ml) ground cloves
1 tsp. (5 ml) ground ginger
1 cup (250 ml) whipping cream
1 Tbsp. (25 ml) vanilla

Grease only the sides of a 10-inch (25 cm) spring-form pan. Crumble gingersnap cookies and combine with 2 Tbsps (50 ml) melted butter and 2 Tbsps (50 ml) white sugar. Press crust onto the bottom of pan.

Preheat oven to 425° F (220° C). In a large bowl, beat cream cheese, sugar, eggs and yolks. Add flour and spices. Beat in cream cheese and vanilla. Add mashed pumpkin and mix thoroughly. Pour into prepared crust and bake for 15 minutes. Place a pan filled with water in the oven to prevent cheesecake from cracking.

Reduce oven to 275° F (135° C), and bake for one hour. Turn off heat and leave to cool in the oven overnight with the door propped slightly open. This also helps to prevent cracking.

Top with whipping cream and slivered almonds (optional). Serve hot, cold or just slightly warm. Makes 12 generous servings.

RADISHES

Most people are familiar with the radish as a round, red vegetable about the size of a large marble. But radishes grow in a surprising array of hues: black, purple or amber; green and white with red flesh; and even more exotic, green and white with white flesh and a reddish-purple, star-like centre. A long white Oriental radish called a daikon is also gaining popularity. This type grows much larger than traditional radishes, has carrot-like roots which are used like turnips, and stores well.

Radishes are one of the quickest crops from sowing to harvest: they are ready for eating from four to five weeks after seeding. For this reason, their seed can be mixed with that of slower-growing vegetables like carrots or parsnips, to mark the rows. As you pick them, room is left for the other crops to mature. Radishes are a good choice for the most impatient gardeners — children!

RECOMMENDED VARIETIES

Cherry Belle • bright red, very round, tasty roots; mild flavour.
White Icicle • Long French (French Breakfast) type; white, crisp, tender cylindrical roots, up to 6 inches (15 cm) long.

Cherry Belle

White Icicle

BEFORE YOU PLANT

• Plant in a rich, moist, well-drained soil. The key to mild, crisp, juicy radishes is to grow them as quickly as possible.

• Mix your radish seed with the seed of carrots, beets, onions, lettuce, parsnips or cucumbers. Radish seed takes only four to eight days to germinate, approximately half the time of most vegetables. Because they grow so quickly, the radishes can be harvested long before they create too much competition for the other vegetables which were seeded with them.

Radishes contain Vitamin C and minerals.

WHEN TO PLANT

• Begin to sow radishes as soon as ground can be worked in spring, and continue sowing at one to two-week intervals until mid-July.

HOW MUCH TO PLANT

• For a continuous supply of tender, juicy radishes throughout the summer, sow a handful of seed every week. Summer crops can be sown in a lightly shaded area of the garden.

PLANTING METHODS

• Sow seeds to the depth of the fingernail on your index finger.

• Plant three short rows, about 2 feet (60 cm) long and spaced 2 inches (5 cm) apart. Or, scatter seed in a 1 foot wide (30 cm) band to create a miniature meadow of radishes.

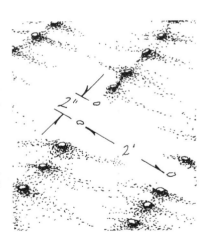

GROWING TIPS

• Keep radishes well-watered: they will grow steadily and taste better. Dry spells cause roots to become hot and woody.

HARVESTING

• Begin to harvest radishes as soon as they are big enough to eat.

• Once radishes have reached full-size, prompt harvest is important. Radishes are at their peak for only a few days. Once they are ready, harvest the entire crop, wash and store in the refrigerator. By the time they are consumed, another crop will be ready for harvest in the garden. Radishes left too long in the ground are apt to attract root maggots.

STORAGE

• Wash radishes and store inside plastic bags in the crisper drawer of the refrigerator. They will stay crisp and in good condition for several weeks.

PROBLEMS

My radishes have a funny taste and a texture similar to styrofoam. What is wrong?

Hot, dry conditions can cause radishes to become pithy and hot-tasting. They may split or develop hollow insides. Prevent these problems by planting early in the season, sowing successive crops in small amounts, and spacing radishes closely together. Water during periods of drought.

Radishes produce a lot of top growth when given too much nitrogen.

RUTABAGA

Rutabagas (Swedes, Swede turnips, winter turnips) are often confused with turnips (summer turnips). Rutabagas are related to and cultivated in the same manner as turnips, but differ in many other ways. Rutabaga roots are sweeter, shaped like large beets, and often creamy yellow inside and out with a purple crown. Turnips are smaller, rounder, white-fleshed summer vegetables. They are fast-growing, and cannot be stored for long periods. Rutabagas are hardier, take up to twice as long to mature, and store as well as potatoes, under proper conditions. People often mean rutabagas when they say turnips.

RECOMMENDED VARIETIES

Alta Sweet • deep yellow flesh; more mildly-flavoured than most varieties; large, globe-shaped roots with small tops.

BEFORE YOU PLANT

- Rutabagas do best in a soil that is loose but not too rich. Too much nitrogen can cause puny or split roots and big green tops.

- Never add fresh manure; it may produce rough, hairy roots and will cause forks and splits. If fresh manure has been added to the soil, wait until the next growing season to plant any root crop; well-rotted manure is fine.

Rutabagas are a good source of dietary fibre.

WHEN TO PLANT

- Rutabagas are fast-growing, but need a long growing season to develop large roots. Sow as soon as the ground can be worked for a late summer crop, and in the first week of June for a fall crop.

HOW MUCH TO PLANT

- One large rutabaga provides about three servings at a meal.

PLANTING METHODS

- Sow seed at fingertip depth.
- Sprinkle seed thinly along single rows.

GROWING TIPS

- Thin plants when they are 3 to 4 inches (7.5 - 10 cm) tall, to about 4 to 6 inches (10 - 15 cm) apart. Use the thinnings in the kitchen, as greens.

HARVESTING

Thin plants when 3 - 4 inches high.

- Rutabagas are at their best when the roots are between the size of a tennis ball and a softball.

- Pull the roots as needed throughout the fall, and lift the entire crop after a late fall frost. Frost will sweeten the roots.

Experiment with these herbs when using rutabagas in the kitchen: basil, dill, ginger, mint, nutmeg, parsley.

STORAGE

- Cut tops off to within 1 inch (2.5 cm) of the root, wash and place inside perforated plastic bags to prevent moisture loss. Rutabagas store well in this manner for several weeks, if kept in a cool, moist place. For longer storage, up to several months, keep rutabagas in a humid area, with temperatures near freezing.
- Use within one week if kept at room temperature.

PROBLEMS

What are common problems with growing rutabaga?

*Rutabagas and turnips are often severely attacked by root maggots. With turnip crops, root maggots can strike two or even three times in a season; with other vegetables, the first attack is usually the last. See **Cabbage** for methods of control, and try to plant turnip crops in slightly sandy soil. Black, rich soils attract root maggots to a much greater extent than do light, sandy soils.*

Rutabaga

> Rutabagas can be baked, scalloped or French fried, like potatoes. Serve raw sticks on a vegetable platter, or boil cut pieces uncovered for about half an hour until tender, drain and serve with butter, lemon juice and chopped parsley. Try them mashed and mixed with any proportion of mashed potatoes. Serve with lots of chopped parsley, or sour cream and a light dusting of nutmeg.

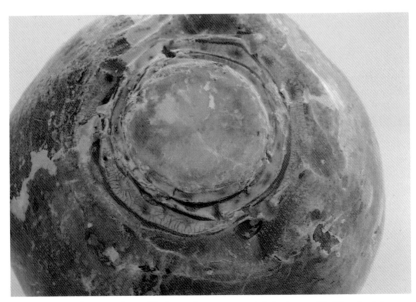

Rutabagas are often coated in a thin layer of wax, to extend their storage life. Waxed rutabagas can simply be kept in a kitchen cupboard, as the wax prevents their dehydration.

SPINACH

Spinach is easy to grow and thrives in relatively cool temperatures: the key to growing great greens is in timing the planting. I recommend growing at least one spring and one fall crop. Spinach is at its most nutritious when raw, but still rich in vitamins and minerals if cooked quickly. Steam it covered for just a few minutes, drain well, and add butter, salt and pepper. Sprinkle with white vinegar or lemon juice for added flavour.

RECOMMENDED VARIETIES

Melody • hybrid; slightly crinkled (semi-savoy) leaves; easy to clean; the type you often find in supermarkets.
Longstanding Bloomsdale • a traditional variety; the most crumpled leaves of any variety (savoy); harder to clean.

Melody

*Longstanding
Bloomsdale*

BEFORE YOU PLANT

• Spinach requires rich soil and an abundant supply of nitrogen. Spread blood meal or a high nitrogen fertilizer along the row to encourage a larger, more succulent crop.

• Spinach is one of the few vegetables that can withstand partial shade. Crops in a slightly shaded area will grow somewhat more slowly, but also be slower to **bolt** to seed in the heat of the summer. Consider planting spinach between rows of taller-growing vegetables, particularly for late spring sowings.

Spinach is an excellent source of vitamins A and C, and minerals.

WHEN TO PLANT

• Plant as early as possible in the spring, and again in mid-July, for a late harvest of fresh green leaves. If you are very fond of spinach, sow more often, allowing two weeks between seedings.

• Spinach stays at its best longer when the days are fairly short; long, hot summer days cause it to bolt quickly. Cover the plants with an old blanket or towel if there is a risk of frost.

HOW MUCH TO PLANT

• It is better to sow small amounts more often than a larger amount at a single seeding. A 5-foot (150 cm) row is usually adequate for four to five meals.

PLANTING METHODS

• Sow seed to a depth slightly less than your first knuckle.

• Plant a single row, thickly seeded, or scatter the seed in a 1-foot-wide (30 cm) band to create a miniature meadow of spinach. This method works well in a small garden.

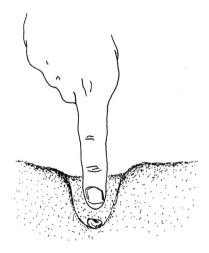

• Create a small salad garden by mixing spinach and leaf lettuce seed, and sowing them together into a sunny area of your flower bed, in mid-May. The salad patch will add a pretty splash of colour to the garden, and as it is used up, simply plant flowers into the space left in the bed. Spinach also grows well and looks attractive in a patio container.

• Experiment with a fall seeding, in late October. Sow twice as thickly and twice as deep as you would in spring, to compensate for the loss of seed viability over the winter months. Prepare the ground well before seeding. You will have spinach ready for eating from two to four weeks earlier than a spring-planting.

GROWING TIPS

- Water every three or four days during dry spells.
- Faced with any sort of stress, spinach is likely to bolt to seed. Warm weather, inadequate moisture, and rapid temperature changes may cause it to become bitter.

HARVESTING

- Harvest spinach while the leaves are young and tender. Pull entire plants up, snip off the roots and put them into your compost bin.
- If possible, harvest spinach on the same day that you plan to use it.

STORAGE

- Wrap unwashed spinach in paper towels and store inside plastic bags in the refrigerator; use within four days.
- Before using, wash carefully in warm water to dislodge any dirt clinging to the leaves. Drain well.

Experiment with these herbs when using spinach in the kitchen: anise, basil, caraway, chervil, chives, cinnamon, dill, mint, rosemary, thyme.

PROBLEMS

What causes spinach to bolt to seed so quickly?

Long, hot days trigger spinach **bolt**. *Short, cool days allow spinach more time to produce leaves before going to seed. Spinach is best planted early in spring with successive small plantings that can be consumed while the crop is at its prime. Some varieties are more resistant to bolting than others.*

Melody is a semi-savoy type spinach.

SQUASH

There are two basic types of squash: summer and winter. Summer squashes include zucchini; however, because zucchini is so popular, we have given it a chapter of its own. Other types of summer squashes have a wide range of colours and shapes, including: white, green and yellow scallops or pattypans; cylindrical, striped cocozelles; and yellow straightneck and crookneck types. Summer squashes are eaten raw or cooked, when the fruit is immature and has a soft skin.

Winter squashes generally have flesh which is darker orange, less fibrous and higher in sugar and dry matter than either pumpkins or mature summer squash. Winter squashes are hard-shelled, keep for long periods in storage, and are most often prepared for eating by baking in the oven.

RECOMMENDED VARIETIES

Summer squash
Cocozelle • Italian Vegetable Marrow type; green striped; long, slender, cylindrical fruit.
Sundance • crookneck type; bright yellow; very smooth skin; easy to pick.
Scallopini • scallop (patty pan) type; dark green; a delicious gourmet bush-type.
Sunbar • straightneck type; glossy yellow; slightly tapered, cylindrical fruit.
Vegetable Marrow • bush type; snow-white; can be allowed to reach maturity, or picked young as cousa (Lebanese zucchini).

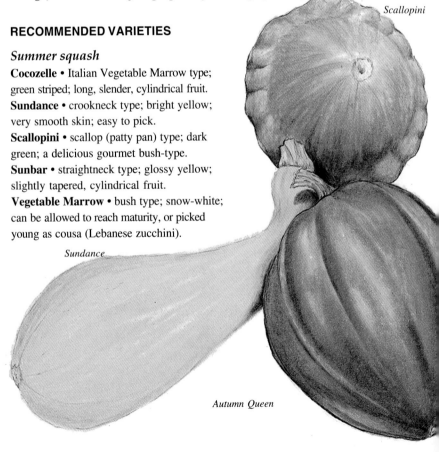

Scallopini

Sundance

Autumn Queen

Winter squash

Autumn Queen • acorn (pepper) type; dark green; a semi-bush type; rich orange flesh with a delicious, fine texture.

Buttercup • one of the best buttercup squashes; dark green; vining; sweet, dry orange flesh; will grow up to 4 pounds (1.8 kg).

Early Butternut Hybrid • the earliest and one of the best butternut types; tan shells, orange flesh; a very productive bush-type; fruit from 1 to 3 pounds (.5 to 1.5 kg).

Warted Hubbard • dark green; vining; attractive, heavily-warted shells; stores very well.

Golden Hubbard • orange-red; vining; moderately-warted.

Vegetable Spaghetti • early-maturing; vining; pale yellow, oblong; a unique type of squash with flesh that separates into spaghetti-like strands when cooked; as delicious and less calories than pasta.

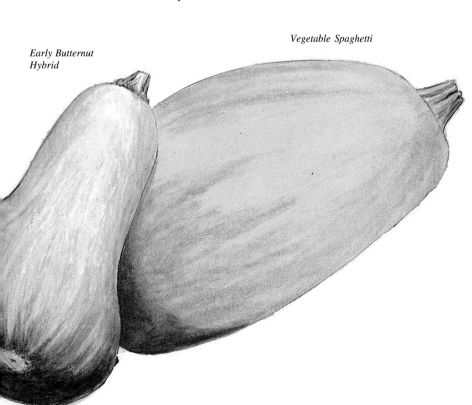

Vegetable Spaghetti

Early Butternut Hybrid

BEFORE YOU PLANT

- The soil should be rich and well-drained. A sunny spot which is sheltered from winds is best.

WHEN TO PLANT

- Squash seed needs warm soil to germinate and root properly. Late May to early June is usually the best time to sow seed.

HOW MUCH TO PLANT

- Two to six plants of summer squash will produce enough for an average family if picked frequently.
- Three or four plants of winter squash is usually adequate.

Squash is a good source of vitamins A and C.

PLANTING METHODS

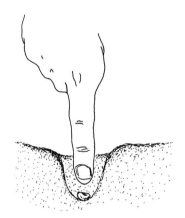

- Sow seeds to the depth of your first knuckle.
- Sow four to five seeds in a hill. Space hills 3 feet (90 cm) apart.
- Almost any bush-type variety of summer squash does splendidly in a large patio container. Winter varieties should be grown in the garden, as they require more room and have an extensive root system.

GROWING TIPS

- To keep vigourous squash vines from taking over your garden, try these ideas:
  - pinch off growing ends of vines after enough fruit has set;
  - direct vines back in towards the plant;
  - plant squash along the edge of the garden and let vines run onto your lawn;
  - weave the vines around your corn patch;
  - with smaller fruited varieties, try training the plants up a trellis.
- Keep weeds down until the leaves grow large enough to shade them out.
- Water deeply once a week during dry spells. Water around the base of the plants, not over them, and try to do so early in the day to allow plants to dry before nightfall.
- Avoid splashing dirt onto the leaves; many diseases are harboured in the soil and can be transferred to foliage in this manner.
- Stop watering winter types once the vines begin to die.

HARVESTING

Summer Squash

• Harvest regularly to keep the vines producing. Many summer squashes should be picked twice weekly to increase the yield.

• For the best flavour, harvest when young and tender. Pattypan squash is at its best when 3 to 4 inches (7.5 - 10 cm) across. Summer squashes lose some flavour at maturity.

Winter Squash

• Harvest after all vines die or after the first light frost. Flavour is often improved after a light frost, as the sugar content increases.

• The rind should be a deep, solid colour, and hard enough that it cannot easily be pierced by a fingernail. Immature squash will not ripen after picking.

• Harvest on a sunny, dry day, if possible. Cut the vines, leaving some stem. Roll the squash and leave it out to dry for a few hours. Be careful not to bruise the squash, and do not carry it by the handle.

STORAGE

Summer Squash

• Summer squashes are perishable. Refrigerate and use within a week.

Winter Squash

• Winter squash can be stored only if its skin cannot be easily pierced by your thumbnail. Squash stored on a shelf in a cool, dry place will keep for several months. Do not store on a cement floor or in an unheated garage.

PROBLEMS

What causes my winter squash to rot in storage?

Winter squash must be mature in order to store well. Shells must be hard enough that they cannot be easily pierced by a fingernail. Concrete floors cause squash to "sweat", promoting rot, and should never be used as a storage surface for squash. Inspect squash in storage occasionally and immediately destroy any squashes which show signs of rot.

An example of bush varieties of squash growing in the field.

SWISS CHARD

Swiss chard (Seakale beet, leaf beet or simply chard) is a member of the beet family, and is grown for its tasty stems and leaves. The stems are cooked like asparagus, the leaves like spinach. This hardy crop is easy to grow and decorative enough to be placed in a flower bed.

RECOMMENDED VARIETIES

White King • large, thick, white ribs; deeply ruffled, dark green leaves.
Rhubarb Chard • bright ruby red stems and veins; dark green leaves.

White King

Rhubarb Chard

BEFORE YOU PLANT

• Swiss chard grows well in moderately fertile soil and withstands light shade.

WHEN TO PLANT

• Plant in the first week of May. Be cautious about sowing red chard too early, as these plants may bolt to seed if exposed to cold spring temperatures.

HOW MUCH TO PLANT

• Plant only a single row, as Swiss chard regrows after its leaves are cut for harvest.

Swiss chard is a good source of Vitamin A and iron.

PLANTING METHODS

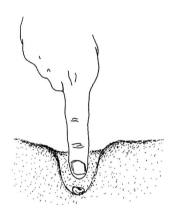

• Sow seeds to the depth of the nail of your index finger.

• Sprinkle seed in a single row, wide band or square.

• Experiment with a fall seeding, in late October. Sow twice as thickly and twice as deep, to compensate for loss of viability over the winter months. The Swiss chard will be ready for eating two to four weeks earlier than a spring-planted crop.

GROWING TIPS

• Swiss chard needs to be thinned only if you want big stalks to grow. To thin, allow 4 to 6 inches (10 - 15 cm) between plants, and bring the young plants you pull to the kitchen, to use in soups and salads.

HARVESTING

• Cut away the leaves at the base of the plant, as needed. New leaves will grow.

STORAGE

• Store inside plastic bags in the refrigerator; use within four days.

PROBLEMS

What are common problems with growing Swiss chard?

Swiss chard is relatively problem-free. It matures long before many of the major insect pests develop. However, because it grows so quickly, it is best to plant smaller amounts, which can be consumed while the crop is at its prime.

TOMATOES

Tomatoes are perhaps the most popular vegetable for the home gardener. People who grow no other vegetables usually have a tomato plant or two tucked in amongst the flowers or growing in a patio container. This is due, in part, to the extreme difference in taste between a vine-ripened, home-grown tomato and the flavourless, mealy-textured tomato often found in grocery stores. Another factor is the challenge of growing the "perfect tomato", a consideration which is, I think, particularly appealing to men: many of our male customers are fussier than women in selecting plants, and like to boast more often about their results.

There are two basic types of tomato plants: determinate and indeterminate. Determinate plants are the bush type, which set all their fruit within a relatively short period of time, do not need to be pruned, and grow well in a cage. Indeterminate plants are tall-growing, produce fruit throughout the growing season, and need to be staked or grown against a trellis. These plants need to be pruned.

RECOMMENDED VARIETIES

Super Fantastic • indeterminate; extra-large tomatoes; very meaty, nicely-shaped, beefsteak tomatoes; an "outdoor" tomato that also grows well in a greenhouse; high yields; matures mid-season.

Lemon Boy

Super Fantastic

Sweet 100

Floramerica • determinate; large tomatoes; the best bush-type beefsteak tomato; top-quality fruit; superb fresh, canned or juiced; matures mid-season.

Counter • indeterminate; medium-sized tomatoes; very round, uniform, high-quality fruit; heavy yields; greenhouse-type; also grows well in a garden; resistant to blossom-end rot; matures early to mid-season.

Early Girl • indeterminate; medium-sized tomatoes; the earliest slicing tomato; magnificent flavour; early-maturing.

Lemon Boy • indeterminate; medium-sized tomatoes; the best yellow tomato; low acid, mild-tasting; high yields; matures mid-season.

Tumbler • determinate; small tomatoes; excellent for growing in hanging baskets and patio containers; delicious, round fruit, slightly larger than cherry tomatoes; needs lots of water and fertilizer; outstanding yields; matures mid-season.

Sweet 100 • indeterminate; cherry tomatoes; the highest-yielding cherry tomato; superb in large patio containers and in the garden; tremendous amounts of sweet fruit borne in trusses; up to 20 tomatoes per truss; matures early to mid-season.

Tiny Tim • determinate; cherry tomatoes; a dwarf plant that is ideal for patio containers and window boxes; great for children's gardens; early-maturing.

Mamma Mia • determinate; paste tomatoes; a variety our Italian customers shop for by name; up to three times the yield of other paste tomato varieties; exceptional for sauces, canning and fresh eating; matures early to mid-season.

Mamma Mia

Early Girl

BEFORE YOU PLANT

- Tomatoes do best in a warm, sunny, sheltered spot. Choose a site which receives about eight hours of sun each day. A south-facing location near a wall is perfect.
- If you are planting in containers, top them up with fresh potting soil each year for the best results.

WHEN TO PLANT

- Take a chance on an earlier crop by planting a few tomatoes in early May, if the weather is good. Choose a sheltered location against a house wall or set hot caps over the seedlings, and be prepared to cover the plants if there is a risk of frost.
- Put the majority of your plants into the garden from the middle to the end of May. Growing plants that mature at different times will provide ripe tomatoes over a longer period.

HOW MUCH TO PLANT

- Yields vary tremendously with seasonal conditions. In general, two dozen plants will provide enough tomatoes for salads, cooking, canning, freezing and eating fresh from late June to September.
- A bush (determinate) tomato plant needs up to twice as much room as a staked, tall-growing (indeterminate) plant. If you have limited space, the latter is probably a better choice.
- Generally, indeterminate plants have higher yields, but they require more work throughout the growing season.

A tiny bit of sugar sprinkled over sliced ripe tomatoes really enhances the flavour. For a different but equally pleasing taste, top with fresh chopped basil.

PLANTING METHODS

- Prepare a hole for each plant. Pinch off some of the lower leaves and place plants into the holes, just slightly deeper than they were growing in their original containers. Deep planting is best since roots will form along any part of the stem that is buried, resulting in a stronger plant.
- If your plants are long-stemmed and lanky, *trench planting* is the best method. Pinch off the lower leaves and lay the entire plant horizontally in a shallow trench. Cover the stem with 2 to 3 inches (5 - 7.5 cm) of soil, leaving just the top cluster of leaves above the surface.

Use a hoe to create a shallow trench.

- Roots will form all along the buried stem, enabling the plant to better absorb water and nutrients. Since more roots are formed near the warm soil surface, the plant quickly becomes vigourous, resulting in increased yields and earlier maturity.
- Plant indeterminate varieties 18 to 24 inches (45 - 60 cm) apart and use stakes to support them. If you plan to let determinate plants spread, space them 36 to 48 inches (90 - 120 cm) apart; 36 inches (90 cm) is adequate room for caged plants. Allow 36 inches (90 cm) between rows.

GROWING TIPS

- An even, adequate supply of water is most important during early fruit sizing. Inconsistent moisture (allowing the plant to dry out and then soaking it) or too little watering can result in smaller fruit and blossom-end rot. Water heavily at least twice a week, and every day without fail if the weather is hot and dry.
- Fertilize regularly. Use a *starter* 10-52-10 fertilizer weekly for the first three weeks after transplanting. Thereafter, I recommend feeding tomatoes every time you water, with just a pinch of 20-20-20 fertilizer added to the watering can.

Cages

- Determinate varieties take up less room and grow well in cages, although you can just leave them to grow free. Caged tomato plants develop lots of foliage, providing protective shade for ripening fruit. Tomatoes inside cages are held high above the ground, safe from slugs and soil-born diseases.
- Set cages over the tomatoes immediately after transplanting and push them firmly into the ground. Once the cages are in place, the tomatoes are virtually maintenance-free.
- Make a tight circle of 1-foot (30 cm) high black felt paper or dark plastic around the outside of the cage at ground level. The black paper will heat the tomato plants (important early in the season) and also protect the plants from winds.
- Uncaged or free-growing tomato plants take up more space in the garden — at least 1 square yard (1 m^2) for each plant.

Staking Tomatoes

- Staking indeterminate plants saves space: you can grow more plants in a given area. Vines and fruit are held off the ground, safe from slugs, dust and soil-borne diseases. Staked plants are easier to work around, the fruit is easier to pick and often ripens earlier.
- When staking, try to set the support on the prevailing downwind side of the plant, so that the plant will be protected against the support in strong winds.

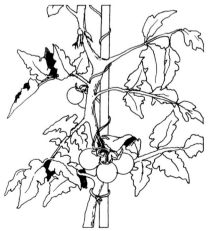

As the plants grow, tie loosely to a stake.

- Put the stakes in immediately after transplanting. Drive them about 1 foot (30 cm) deep in the soil, approximately 3 to 5 inches (7.5 - 12.5 cm) away from the plant. If you have trench-planted tomatoes, do not put the stake on the root side of the plant.

To easily peel skins from ripe tomatoes, place them into a bowl and pour boiling water over top to completely cover. Leave one minute, drain and run under cold water. The skins will split and slide off effortlessly. The riper the tomatoes, the better this method works.

- As the plant grows, tie it **loosely** to the stake. Use a soft material, such as cut-up nylon stockings, and leave 1 to 2 inches (2.5 - 5 cm) of slack to allow the stem to thicken and grow. Add more ties as required.

Pruning

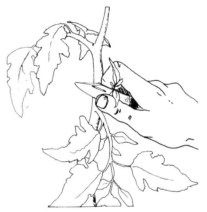

- Only indeterminate varieties need pruning. Pruning tomato plants simply means pinching off the shoots or *suckers* that grow out from the stem, in the crotch right above a leaf branch. If you leave a sucker, it grows into another big stem, taking energy away from fruit production. Tomatoes often ripen slightly earlier on pruned plants.

- Tomato plants grow very quickly when the weather warms up. New suckers are produced all the time. Prune at least twice a week during peak growing season.

Prune suckers with a sharp knife.

Topping

- You can also prune an indeterminate plant if it is outgrowing its support, although the growth can simply be trained to grow back downwards. I like to top my plants towards the end of the growing season when it is preferable for all their energy to be devoted to ripening the tomatoes already on the vine.

Fresh ripe tomatoes are an excellent source of vitamins A and C.

- Greenhouse tomatoes will grow well in an open garden if given an optimum location: very sunny, warm and sheltered. Tomatoes which are not noted as greenhouse types can be grown inside a greenhouse; however, they cannot match the yield of greenhouse tomatoes.

- Try these tips to encourage tomatoes to ripen on the vine late in the season:
  - "Top" indeterminate varieties: remove the top set of leaves to stop the plants from adding height, and allow more energy for ripening existing fruit.
  - Remove all flowers and any tiny tomatoes.
  - If your plants are in containers, move them into the sunniest area.

HARVESTING

- Harvest ripe tomatoes by gently breaking the stem just beyond the fruit at the knuckle.

- If the weather forces you to harvest tomatoes green, pick only the ones which are at least three-quarters of their mature size. Encourage them to ripen indoors by placing them at room temperature, between sheets of newspaper, in a dark area.

Experiment with these herbs when using tomatoes in the kitchen: basil, bay leaf, chives, coriander, dill, garlic, lovage, marjoram, mint, oregano, parsley, rosemary, sage, savory, tarragon, thyme.

STORAGE

- Never store tomatoes in the refrigerator. The cool temperature causes them to lose flavour and texture and they will not last as long as those kept at room temperature. If you like tomatoes chilled, put them in the refrigerator for an hour before serving.

Hotcaps protect tender tomato plants early in the season. As they mature, slit the hotcaps open to allow the plants room to grow.

PROBLEMS

The leaves on my tomato plants are twisted and deformed, and the plants are not growing well.

Twisted, curled or deformed leaves, especially on new growth, are usually the result of weed killers inadvertently sprayed on tomato plants. Severely-damaged plants cannot be saved and should be thrown out. Never apply "weed-and-feed" type fertilizers near tomato plants.

Leaves may also curl or roll up after periods of heavy rain, or when there is a wide variation in day and night temperatures. If disease and pests are absent, do not worry about it. Watering regularly, evenly and thoroughly, planting in rich, well-drained soil, and growing hybrid varieties help to prevent leaf roll.

My plants have pale yellow and greyish-white patches on the fruit and leaves.

This is likely sunscald, caused by excessive exposure to intense sunlight and heat. Plant tomatoes away from white, sun-reflecting walls, or block those walls with a non-reflective covering, such as burlap.

Why are my tomatoes cracking on the vine?

This can be caused by very fast growth, often during a warm, rainy period following a dry spell, especially when fruit is full-size and beginning to turn colour. Keep moisture supply as even as possible throughout the season.

There are unusual swellings and scar-like streaks on my tomatoes.

That sounds like cat-facing, a condition resulting from abnormal floral development, due to abnormally hot or cool weather. The tomatoes are less attractive but still edible.

What causes black or brown rotten spots on the bottom of tomatoes?

This is a condition called blossom-end rot, caused by water stress or calcium deficiency due to poor or heavy clay soils, or irregular or inadequate watering, especially during a period of quick growth. Cut off affected portions; the remainder of the tomato is fine for eating. Improve watering practices to save developing fruit.

Prevent blossom-end rot by watering regularly and evenly. Plant in rich soil. Feed with a balanced fertilizer containing calcium. Purchase hybrid varieties.

Tomato Marmalade

A recipe my mother used to make, and a delicious change from citrus marmalade.

12 to 16 ripe tomatoes
2 lemons
1/4 cup (60 ml) cider vinegar
1 Tbsp. (25 ml) finely chopped fresh ginger
3 cups (750 ml) sugar

Peel and coarsely chop tomatoes. Wash lemons, cut up and chop finely. Combine all ingredients in a large heavy saucepan. Bring to a boil over medium heat, reduce heat and cook gently, leave uncovered until thick, about two hours. Ladle into hot sterilized jars and seal. Makes about four 8-ounce (225 g) jars.

TURNIPS

Turnips are sometimes referred to as summer turnips to differentiate them from rutabagas, which are often called winter turnips. True turnips have more tender greens, grow faster than their larger winter cousins, and taste delicious both raw and cooked. A young turnip can be eaten like an apple.

RECOMMENDED VARIETIES

Purple Top White Globe • like the name says, bright purple on top and creamy white below; round smooth roots.
White Lady • matures almost twice as quickly as most turnips; smaller, tasty roots which are white inside and out; often more prone to root maggots than other types.

White Lady

Purple Top White Globe

BEFORE YOU PLANT

• Turnips grow well in a wide range of soil conditions. I prefer to plant in a slightly sandy soil, because the roots are cleaner when pulled.

WHEN TO PLANT

• Plant twice if you really like this vegetable, first in mid-April, and again in late July for a fall harvest.

HOW MUCH TO PLANT

• A 10-foot (3 m) row usually yields about 25 pounds (11 kg) of turnips.

Try this trick in the kitchen: put raw turnips in the freezer a few days before you are ready to use them. Take out of the freezer a few hours before cooking — they will peel easily and slice like butter.

PLANTING METHODS

• Sow at fingertip depth.

• Sow thickly in rows spaced about 2 feet (60 cm) apart.

• Scatter your seed in a 1-foot-wide (30 cm) band to create a miniature meadow of turnips. This method works very well in a small garden, and for those who like greens.

GROWING TIPS

• If you like greens, do not thin turnips. Leave them crowded and harvest greens when young and tender.

HARVESTING

• Turnips are most tender when harvested at the size of a tennis ball or smaller. Larger roots are often bitter and woody.

• Tiny turnips, from 1 to 2 inches (2.5 - 5 cm) in diameter, are tender and mild with a slightly spicy flavour, like a radish. These turnips are wonderful eaten raw.

Experiment with these herbs when using turnips in the kitchen: basil, dill, ginger, mint, nutmeg, parsley, paprika.

STORAGE

• Use turnips within one week if they are stored at room temperature; use within several weeks if kept in a cool, humid place.

Turnip roots are a good source of vitamins. The greens are rich in vitamins A and C.

PROBLEMS

What are common insect problems with growing turnips?

Aside from root maggot attacks, turnips are a relatively trouble-free crop. See **Cabbage** *for methods of controlling root maggots.*

What causes turnips to split?

Turnips may split during periods of fluctuating moisture. Split roots are more prone to becoming infected with root rot diseases. Water turnip plants consistently and thoroughly throughout the growing season to reduce the incidence of splitting.

Turnips

Serve turnips grated in salads, with a dip on a vegetable platter or boiled until tender and flavoured simply with butter, salt and pepper. Try them as an alternative to potatoes around roasts, or serve them glazed with butter, sugar and paprika, and topped with chopped parsley.

Purple Top White Globe and White Lady turnips.

ZUCCHINI

Zucchini grows quickly and produces a large amount of small fruit if harvested regularly, or a lesser amount of enormous fruit if harvested less often. Its uses in the kitchen are varied, from breads to ratatouille. Even the blossoms are edible, and can be stuffed, baked and served alone or as a platter garnish. I like zucchini best when it is lightly cooked, served raw with a vegetable dip, or thickly sliced and sautéed with onions and butter. Add tomatoes, mushrooms or parmesan cheese to enhance the flavour. Young zucchini does not need to be peeled; its skin and seeds are edible. Use zucchini in any recipe which calls for summer squash.

RECOMMENDED VARIETIES

Super Select • bush-type; dark green with light green flecks; extra-long, evenly shaped fruit; heavy yields.
Gold Rush • bush-type; deep golden-yellow; uniform, smooth, cylindrical fruit; easy to pick.

Super Select

Gold Rush

BEFORE YOU PLANT

- The soil should be rich and well-drained. A sunny spot, protected from winds, is best.

Zucchini is a good source of vitamins A and C.

WHEN TO PLANT

- Sow seed or transplant seedlings into the garden in the last week of May.

HOW MUCH TO PLANT

- Usually two to four plants are sufficient. Zucchini is a heavy yielder — expect about 16 fruit per plant.

PLANTING METHODS

- Sow seeds to the depth of your first knuckle.
- Plant five to seven seeds in a hill.
- For the earliest harvest, start seeds indoors two weeks prior to planting, or buy started plants from a greenhouse.

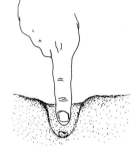

Experiment with these herbs when using zucchini in the kitchen: basil, dill, garlic, marjoram, mint, oregano, rosemary, sage, savory.

GROWING TIPS

- Keep weeds down until the leaves grow large enough to shade them out.
- Water deeply once a week during dry spells. Water around the base of the plants, not over them, and try to do so early in the day to allow plants to dry before nightfall. Avoid splashing dirt onto the leaves; many diseases are harboured in the soil and can be transferred to foliage in this manner.

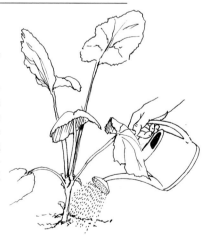

*Be careful to water the **base** of the plants.*

HARVESTING

- Harvest regularly to keep the vines producing. Zucchini should be picked twice weekly to increase the yield.

- For the best flavour, harvest zucchini young. These squashes are at their tender best when picked small, between 4 and 8 inches (10 - 20 cm) long.

- Huge zucchini is impressive more for its size than its taste. When we grew vegetables for farm market sales, we used to hire a young boy or girl for the sole purpose of snipping all zucchini over 12 inches (30 cm) from the vines, thus gaining an extended harvest of tender young fruit. Large zucchini is best used in muffins or breads.

STORAGE

- Zucchini and other summer squashes do not keep well. Refrigerate and use within a week.

PROBLEMS

What causes zucchini to turn mushy and rot?

*Zucchini can suffer from **blossom-end rot** during periods of rapid soil moisture fluctuation. The symptom of this problem is collapsed, rotting fruit, particularly at the blossom end. Regular watering and the addition of bonemeal to the soil around the base of the plants helps prevent this condition.*

Zucchini this size is at its tender best.

APPENDIX I

Vegetable	Temperature	Humidity	Storage Life
Asparagus	32°F/0°C	High	2-3 weeks
Beans	40-45°F/ 5-7°C	High	7-10 days
Beets, bunched	32°F/0°C	High	10-14 days
Beets, topped	32°F/0°C	High	4-6 months
Broccoli	32°F/0°C	High	10-14 days
Brussels sprouts	32°F/0°C	High	3-5 weeks
Cabbage, early	32°F/0°C	High	3-6 weeks
Cabbage, late	32°F/0°C	High	5-6 months
Carrots, bunched	32°F/0°C	High	2 weeks
Carrots, mature	32°F/0°C	High	7-9 months
Carrots, immature	32°F/0°C	High	4-6 weeks
Cauliflower	32°F/0°C	High	3-4 weeks
Celeriac	32°F/0°C	High	6-8 months
Celery	32°F/0°C	High	2-3 months
Corn	32°F/0°C	High	5-8 days
Cucumber	50-55°F/10-13°C	High	10-14 days
Eggplant	45-55°F/7-13°C	High	1 week
Garlic	32°F/0°C	Medium	6-7 months
Kale	32°F/0°C	High	2-3 weeks
Kohlrabi	32°F/0°C	High	2-3 months
Leeks	32°F/0°C	High	2-3 months
Lettuce	32°F/0°C	High	2-3 weeks
Melon, cantaloupe	36-40°F/2-5°C	High	5-15 days
Melon, honeydew	45°F/7°C	High	3 weeks
Melon, watermelon	50-60°F/10-15°C	High	2-3 weeks
Onions, dry	32°F/0°C	Medium	1-8 months
Onions, green	32°F/0°C	High	3-4 weeks
Parsnips	32°F/0°C	High	4-6 months
Peas	32°F/0°C	High	1-2 weeks
Pepper, hot (dry)	32-50°F/0-10°C	Medium	6 months
Pepper, sweet	45-55°F/7-13°C	High	2-3 weeks
Potato	(1)	High	5-10 months
Pumpkins	50-55°F/10-13°C	Medium	2-3 months
Radish	32°F/0°C	High	3-4 weeks
Rutabaga	32°F/0°C	High	4-6 months
Spinach	32°F/0°C	High	10-14 days
Squash, summer	40-50°F/5-10°C	High	1-2 weeks
Squash, winter	50°F/10°C	Medium	(2)
Swiss chard	32°F/0°C	High	10-14 days
Tomatoes, mature green	55-70°F/13-21°C	High	1-3 weeks
Tomatoes, firm ripe	45-50°F/7-10°C	High	4-7 days
Turnips	32°F/0°C	High	4-5 months
Turnips, greens	32°F/0°C	High	10-14 days
Zucchini	40-50°F/5-10°C	High	1-2 weeks

High humidity *means a relative humidity from 90 to 100%.* **Medium humidity** *means a relative humidity from 50 to 70%. All vegetables should be stored in a well-ventilated area.*

(1) Spring- or summer-harvested potatoes are usually not stored. Fall-harvested potatoes should be cured at 50-60°F (10-15°C) and high relative humidity for ten to 14 days. Temperatures should then be gradually lowered to 40-50°F (5-10°C).

(2) Winter squash varieties differ in storage life.

INDEX

A

arugula 30
Asparagus 13, 16, 19, 34-37

B

Beans 14, 16-19, 24, 28, 31-33, 38-41
Beets 14, 16, 17, 19, 42-45
bolting to seed 135
Broccoli 16, 19, 23, 49-51

C

Cabbages 16, 18, 19, 23, 26, 52-55
Cantaloupes *(see melons)*
Carrots 14, 16, 18, 19, 20, 25, 33, 56-59
Celeriac 16, 19 23, 64-66
Celery 14, 16, 19, 23, 26, 67-69
Chives 28, 30, 47, 73, 116
    garlic chives 82
compost 18, 41, 61, 71, 90
Corn 13, 16-19, 26, 70-73
crop rotation 18, 39, 47, 53, 71, 83, 113, 118
cross-pollination 71, 72
Cucumbers 16-19, 23, 26, 28, 31, 32, 74-78

D

Daikon *(see Radishes)*
disease 19, 22, 26-28, 32, 39, 41, 78,
    101, 121, 126
    black scurf 122
    blossom-end rot 25, 148, 154
    common scab 118, 121
    potato scab 118
    powdery mildew 32, 113
    root rot 8, 113, 151
    rust 37, 41

E-F

erosion 19
Eggplant 16, 19, 23, 31, 79-81
endive 30
fertilizer 21, 22, 24, 36, 75, 99, 145
    blood meal 26, 134
    bonemeal 19, 21, 35, 53, 83, 85, 97,
        118, 154
    dispenser 24

nitrogen 16, 24, 39, 41, 75, 84,
    121, 131
phosphorous 16, 24, 35
potassium 16, 24, 75
weed-and-feed 148
frost 12, 13, 14, 15, 23, 39, 51, 53,
    57, 58, 65, 68, 72, 83, 87, 90, 93,
    109, 111, 119, 131, 134, 139, 144
fungicide 21, 22, 24, 39, 71, 111

G

gardening methods
    children 32, 33, 89, 127
    container 13, 30, 31, 76, 80, 96, 99,
        105, 115, 138, 142, 146
    intensive 32
    square foot 32
    vertical 32
Garlic 16, 19, 31, 47, 81, 82-85
germination 20, 21, 23, 39

H-I

herbs 28, 30, 31
hot caps 23, 75, 99, 100, 144
humus *(see organic matter)*
inoculants 39, 111
insecticide 27-29, 45. *(see also pesticide)*
    bacillus thuringiensis (BT) 28, 48
    chemical 28
    diatomaceous earth 28, 97
    diazinon 22, 51
    garlic, as repellant 47, 81, 84, 116
    insecticidal soap 28, 116
    marigolds, as repellants 28, 80, 81, 115
    onion, as repellant 73, 105
    organic controls 28, 97
    pyrethrum 29, 73
    rotenone 29, 45, 73, 81
intercropping 18
irrigation 26

K-L

Kale 16, 19, 86-89
Kohlrabi 16, 19, 33, 89-91
lacewings 28
ladybugs 28, 116
Leeks 16, 19, 23, 92-94

BIBLIOGRAPHY

Hortus Third. New York, NY: MacMillan Publishing, 1976

Rodale's Illustrated Encyclopaedia of Herbs. Emmaus, PA: Rodale Press, 1987

Campbell, Stu. *Let It Rot: The Gardener's Guide to Composting.* Pownal, VT: Storey Communications, Inc., 1990

Harris, Marjorie. *Ecological Gardening: Your Path to a Healthy Garden.* Toronto, ON: Random House, 1991

Riotte, Louise. *Carrots Love Tomatoes.* Pownal, VT: Storey Communications Inc.,1975

Wyman, Donald. *Wyman's Gardening Encyclopaedia.* 3rd ed. New York, NY: MacMillan, 1986

Recommended Periodicals

Gardens West
1090 W. 8th Avenue, Box 1680
Vancouver, BC V6B 3W8

Harrowsmith
7 Queen Victoria Road
Camden East, Ontario K0K 1J0

National Gardening
180 Flynn Avenue
Burlington, VT 05401 USA

Organic Gardening
33 East Minor Street
Emmaus, PA 18098 USA

ABOUT THE AUTHOR

Lois Hole and her husband Ted started selling vegetables out of their red barn over 30 years ago; today Hole's Greenhouse & Gardens Ltd. is one of the largest greenhouse & garden centres in Alberta. It still remains a family business, owned and operated by Lois, Ted, their sons Bill and Jim, and Bill's wife Valerie.

Lois was born and raised in rural Saskatchewan, later moving to Edmonton, Alberta. She attained a degree in Music from the Toronto Conservatory of Music (ATCM). Neither she nor Ted had lived on a farm before starting Hole's but soon were growing grain and raising livestock. Their first vegetable garden began out of necessity.

Lois is often asked to talk and share her expertise with various groups and non-profit organizations. She is known for her enthusiastic involvement in all that she does, and is a familiar face in the greenhouses to many customers who seek out her friendly advice and gardening tips.

Lois and Ted continue to live and work on the same site that they started out on, by the river in St. Albert.

Gardeners Around the World Enjoy Lois Hole's Gardening Series!

Recipient of the
Professional Plant Growers Association 1995 Educational Media Award

Lois Hole's Perennial Favorites

by Lois Hole with Jill Fallis

Drawing on her nearly 40 years' experience in gardening and operating a major greenhouse, Lois Hole has chosen 100 perennial plants for their beauty and hardiness. With common sense and practical wisdom, she tells you how to easily transform any patch of earth into a spectacular garden. *Perennial Favorites* features more than 430 color photographs plus notes on flower colors, height ranges and blooming periods. Packed with straightfoward tips on planting strategies and solving common problems.

5.5" x 8.5" • 352 pages • over 430 color photographs
Softcover • $19.95 CDN • $15.95 US• ISBN 1-55105-056-0

> *"With Lois Hole's* Perennial Favorites *in hand, gardeners will find it's easy as picking daisy petals to look for a favorite flower and find out how to grow it."*
> —Susan Jones, HomeStyle Editor, *St. Albert Gazette*
> *"Another great book...Easy to read, easy to look up plants and some good ideas and tips!"*
> —Brian & Karen Smith, Owners, Woodlea Nurseries, England
> Past Chairman of British Bedding and Pot Plant Association

Lois Hole's Bedding Plant Favorites

by Lois Hole with Jill Fallis

Turn your bare patch of soil into a glorious garden full of color with annual flowers and advice from Lois Hole, gardening expert and greenhouse operator. This book is bursting with ideas about how to make your favorite flowers thrive. Read how to extend your garden into your home with flower drying, bouquet arranging and fragrance ideas. Lois's good advice helps make your gardening easy, successful and enjoyable!

5.5" x 8.5" • 272 pages • over 350 color photographs
Softcover • $19.95 CDN • $15.95 US• ISBN 1-55105-039-0

Lois Hole's Tomato Favorites

by Lois Hole with Jill Fallis

Home-grown tomatoes are one of the great joys of our gardens. Lois Hole provides you with all the secrets of a great tomato harvest, including planting and growing for the entire season, growing large tomatoes, treating tomato problems and how to extend the growing season. Richly illustrated and accompanied by tomato facts and folklore, and organized by size for easy reference, *Tomato Favorites* includes sumptuous recipes of renowned chefs from world-class restaurants and from the kitchens of devoted tomato fans.

> *"This author's collective attributes, from gardening to writing (and several in between), touched with an aura of sincere warmth and affection for the subject she loves so much, and integrated with some solid, down-to-earth tomato gardening advice, all kindle together and radiate profusely from the pages."*
> —Bob Ambrose, Publisher, *The Tomato Club Newsletter*

5.5" x 8.5" • 160 pages • over 258 color photographs
Softcover • $16.95 CDN • $12.95 US • ISBN 1-55105-068-4

Praise for Lois Hole's Gardening Series

> *"Beginner and experienced gardeners alike benefit from Lois's years of experience."*
> —Wayne Gale, President, Stokes Seed

Canada
206 10426 81 Avenue
Edmonton AB T6E 1X5
Ph (403) 433-9333
Fax (403) 433-9646

202A 1110 Seymour Street
Vancouver BC V6B 3N3
Ph (604) 687-5555
Fax (604) 687-5575

USA
16149 Redmond Way, #180
Redmond WA 98052
Ph (206) 343-8397